PRAISE FOR

The Complete Marriage Counselor

"If you are frustrated, puzzled, or about to throw in the towel on your marriage, don't. The answers to the difficulties you are experiencing can be found on the pages of this unique book, which draws on the wisdom of the field's top marital therapists. Buy this book and keep it on your nightstand."

—**Michele Weiner-Davis**, MSW, founder of
www.divorcebusting.com and author of *Divorce Busting*

"Imagine having the best of the best couples therapists giving you advice that can save your marriage from disaster, advice that can bring back the sizzle, the romance, the connection that has been lost! *The Complete Marriage Counselor* provides just that. If you have even a hint of trouble brewing in your relationship, don't wait for a minute! Grab this book! This unique guidance could help make or break your marriage."

—**Diana Kirschner, PhD**, author of the bestselling
Love in 90 Days: The Essential Guide to Finding Your Own True Love

"*The Complete Marriage Counselor* does more than give us honest insights from a wide range of counselors on everything from sex to money. And it does more than supplement this with Sherry's thoughtful commentary. It gives us pithy discussion points for those fearful of entering counseling, and second-plus opinions for those already involved. *The Complete Marriage Counselor* is one 'counselor' whose price is right: It may be a recession, but there's no need for depression."

—**Warren Farrell, PhD**, author of
Women Can't Hear What Men Don't Say and
Why Men Are the Way They Are

"Everybody wants to go to the very best professional they can find when they have a problem. Especially when your relationship isn't working, you need guaranteed help fast! Now you can get just that when you read *The Complete Marriage Counselor*. In it you will find the proven advice from experts who have been helping to save marriages across the country. Let them help you transform your relationship and show you how to breathe new life and vitality back into your marriage!"

—**Dr. Jane Greer, DSW, LMFT**, author of
How Could You Do This to Me? Learning to Trust After Betrayal

"So you thought talking to a best friend or having a therapy session or reading Dear Abby was the be-all or end-all . . . try again. *The Complete Marriage Counselor* tops it all. All the best of all the above rolled into one. This book is better than talking to a best friend, better than a therapy session, better than reading Dear Abby. The most wisdom from the top marital therapists in the country and Sherry herself—what a bargain in this economy. Don't leave home without it—this should be the bible beside your bed!"

—**Bonnie Eaker Weil, PhD**, author of bestsellers
Make Up, Don't Break Up: Rescue Your Relationship and Rekindle Your Romance; *Adultery, the Forgivable Sin*; *Financial Infidelity: Seven Steps to Conquering the #1 Relationship Wrecker*

"A major contribution. Sherry Amatenstein offers a wealth of advice at a challenging time when more couples need it more than ever."

—**Keith Ablow, MD**, author of
Living the Truth: Transform Your Life Through the Power of Insight and Honesty

THE
COMPLETE
MARRIAGE
COUNSELOR

Relationship-Saving Advice from America's Top 50+ Couples Therapists

SHERRY AMATENSTEIN, LMSW
FOREWORD BY TINA B. TESSINA, PHD

adamsmedia
Avon, Massachusetts

Published by Adams Media,
a division of F+W Media, Inc.
57 Littlefield Street, Avon, MA 02322. U.S.A.
www.adamsmedia.com

ISBN 10: 1-60550-013-5
ISBN 13: 978-1-60550-013-3

Printed in the United States of America.

10 9 8 7 6 5 4 3 2 1

Library of Congress Cataloging-in-Publication Data
is available from the publisher.

This publication is designed to provide accurate and authoritative information with
regard to the subject matter covered. It is sold with the understanding that the publisher is not engaged in rendering legal, accounting, or other professional advice.
If legal advice or other expert assistance is required, the services of a competent
professional person should be sought.
—From a *Declaration of Principles* jointly adopted by a Committee of the
American Bar Association and a Committee of Publishers and Associations

Many of the designations used by manufacturers and sellers to distinguish their
products are claimed as trademarks. Where those designations appear in this book
and Adams Media was aware of a trademark claim, the designations have been
printed with initial capital letters.

This book is available at quantity discounts for bulk purchases.
For information, call 1-800-289-0963.

DEDICATION

To my parents, Holocaust survivors, married for fifty-three years. Their union was a shining example of what we all strive for. Mom and Dad, you're in the hearts of Barb, Barry, Brittany, Stacey, and me every day.

ACKNOWLEDGMENTS

To everyone inside the pages of this book—the couples and the experts—a heartfelt THANK YOU. This book could not have been written without your passion and wisdom.

To Bob Diforio, my indefatigable agent; Chelsea King and the rest of the gang at Adams Media; Mark Leventhal for his unwavering, loving support, printing, and supply of Bloody Marys; David LaBarca, an ex turned best friend; Amy B., for her invaluable advice and decades-long friendship; Angela Mason, true blue and my female soul mate; Irina Harris for her life-altering insights over the years; Natalie Z. Riccio, PhD, LCSW, and Frances Goldfarb, LCSW, my supervisors respectively at Washington Square Institute and Long Island Consultation Center, for their wisdom and patience; Susan Shapiro, for her faith in me as a writer and therapist; Amy Ginsburg, whose sweetness and steadiness has meant so much; Karen Jones, for help with the website; Paul Kelly, for his kindness and caring over the years; and everyone else who put up with me while I was immersed in this book. And of course to my patients.

CONTENTS

ASTOUNDING WISDOM

If you are in a committed relationship or have had one in the past, you'll recognize the questions couples ask in this book. If you're wondering why you can't sustain a committed relationship, you'll find a lot of answers here. As a therapist in private practice for many years, I encounter these very questions on a daily basis—the couples I work with ask them repeatedly. Using her expertise as a columnist, author, and counselor, Sherry Amatenstein, LMSW, invites well-known authors, therapists, coaches, and counselors to answer them in this enlightening and informative book. As a result, the reader is treated to a very revealing glimpse into the private space of the counseling office, as well as the different approaches of the experts.

Most couples wait far too long before agreeing to go for counseling together. Sometimes, a judge has to mandate counseling or mediation before a couple will seek help. Because marital problems tend to get more entrenched with time, this delay means the couple's habits and attitudes are more ingrained and harder to change, so counseling takes more time and money. *The Complete Marriage Counselor* can make an important difference to real couples by demystifying the advice of the experts and by demonstrating how reasonable and effective that advice can be. Hopefully, anyone reading it to search for answers about his or her relationship questions will be encouraged to seek counseling, if the answers here are not all he or she needs. Sherry includes guidelines for finding counseling at the end of the book.

The advice of the experts quoted here is wise and thoughtful, obviously the result of years of helping struggling couples communicate better, solve problems, create more functional partnerships, and increase the love and intimacy between them. Sherry offers her "take"—her astute recap and analysis of the experts' varied responses to each question and her own advice for the particular situation. The sum total gives you, the reader, several points of view from which to assess the situation and a variety of solutions to apply in your own relationship.

In a couple's counseling session, partners ask about fairness, frustration, sex, intimacy, chores, family dysfunction, betrayal, infidelity, monogamy, privacy, money, parenting, blended families, struggling, time, health, anger, separating, and starting over. Sherry covers all those topics and more. Because these are the major issues most couples struggle with, you'll undoubtedly see snapshots of your own past and present relationships in these pages.

The experts' suggestions clearly show that simple changes can make a very effective difference to a struggling, confused, or concerned couple. The advice here can also be useful to couples who are not struggling but who simply have questions they may not be comfortable sharing with friends and family, or even each other. I also believe it will be a great resource for stimulating conversation between you and your mate. If your mate doesn't read much, try just reading one (carefully chosen) question aloud from this book. Presto! You'll have instant conversation.

As you read, you'll find that this book affords a priceless array of well-known and respected counselors, and reveals that even experts don't always agree. When they don't, Sherry is right there to sort out any confusion.

This book also is useful to me as a therapist, because I often find that backing up my own counsel with the advice of other experts helps my clients to understand the recommendations in a more well-rounded way. I am delighted to see the questions and answers here. I can picture myself pulling out this book when a client is resisting or confused, and reading the advice in these pages aloud, which will accomplish several things: It gives the clients several different points of view from which to view the problem, shows that the experts often agree on what's most important, and helps partners understand the changes in attitude and habit that are necessary to create a relationship that works.

Every counselor in these pages has dedicated his or her life's work to helping couples navigate the often rocky, winding pathways to marital success and satisfaction. Appendix B in the back lists brief bios, books, and the philosophy of each expert. It's an astounding list. The sum total of wisdom, experience, and perspective you will find here will astonish and enlighten you, and definitely benefit your relationship.

—TINA B. TESSINA
Long Beach, California

Tina B. Tessina, PhD, LMFT, also known as "Dr. Romance," is a licensed psychotherapist and author of thirteen books in sixteen languages. Find her on the web at *www.tinatessina.com* and *http://drromance.typepad.com*.

SOMETHING DIFFERENT

- I hate his family. What can I do to get out of seeing them so often?
- Why does she always overspend? Why is he such a cheapskate?
- What are some sexual techniques we can incorporate into our admittedly limited repertoire?
- How can I forgive him for cheating on me?
- Why is the death of our child making us feel more distant from each other?

We've all read books by experts offering "solutions" for couples whose marriages are at or nearing crisis point. Many of those books are extremely valuable. However, *The Complete Marriage Counselor* offers something different. My philosophy in conceiving this project was simple. Why settle for advice from one sage or even two when you can glean the combined wisdom of the country's top marriage counselors in one handy volume? The result is an essential compendium—one-stop shopping for anyone whose relationship could use a little or a lot of help.

There are several wonderful books featuring questions two people should ask themselves and each other before taking the plunge. This volume contains the most pressing post-plunge questions for which longtime couples desperately need down, dirty, and deeply effective answers. Those answers will come not from one or two sources but an assemblage of the most esteemed relationship counselors in the country. Imagine—receive the combined wisdom of sixty-seven experts for much less than the cost of a single therapy session!

Consider that when consulting a physician, most patients go for a second opinion. No matter how wonderful and sound one person's advice is, another opinion can open a window and shed light on an equally valuable perspective. Couples seeking help should have that option, along with a discerning mediator (myself!) to sort through the occasionally conflicting perspectives to pinpoint the most salient answers. For each question, I offer my own two cents. Interspersed throughout the chapters are short, advice-laden profiles. These include Lasting Love, featuring interviews with couples happily married for at least twenty-five years; If I Had a Do-Over, highlighting hard-gained counsel from divorcees; and From the Files of. . . . The latter are case histories shared by counselors detailing how they saved a specific couple's marriage. At the end of each chapter is a Field Report detailing how a couple worked through an impasse that was threatening the marriage.

The therapists participating in my book comprise a Who's Who of the best in the business, including John Gray, PhD; Judy Kuriansky, PhD; Harville Hendrix, PhD; Cloé Madanes, PhD, FAPA; Warren Farrell, PhD; Sue Johnson, EdD; Bonnie Eaker Weil, PhD; Frank Pittman, MD; and Esther Perel. The experts cited here cull from a variety of therapeutic approaches that are based on years of research and practical application. Thus, their techniques work.

- Why doesn't he ever initiate anything? Why do I have to be the one to do everything?
- Can monogamy work?
- Why can't she ever just let anything go—when I want to reconnect and make overtures to her?
- Why can't he just open up and tell me what he's thinking?

Tolstoy famously said, "Happy families are all alike; every unhappy family is unhappy in its own way." The legendary Russian novelist had the equation reversed. In actuality it's the behavior of dysfunctional pairs that can be depressingly similar and predictable. Couples often repeat patterns subconsciously inherited from their parents—for example, always needing to be right or to wrest control from the other person. Consequently, a relentless, repetitive conflict rather than healthy communication becomes many a pair's North Star.

That's not to say this book is meant only for duos that are trapped in seriously dysfunctional hammerlocks. *The Complete Marriage Counselor* can provide a service for those at varying levels of functionality. The communication skills and problem-solving techniques laid out by these pros to handle a multitude of dilemmas can help keep couples on track and/or put back on track those who have derailed.

Many couples exist in a sometimes barely tolerable status quo. Day to day, things seem passable, but come New Year's Eve, the time of annual accounting, one or both secretly wishes, "Gee I wish things were more dynamic between us." No growth, no pain—but no effort, no gain. Then there are the fortunate ones for whom the two words that best describe their marriage are "simply wonderful." Well, wouldn't it be wonderful to find game-saving tips before the game is even in jeopardy?

- My wife is undergoing chemotherapy and I'm frightened she won't make it, but I'm trying to be strong. Should I tell her how scared I am?
- How can I handle her being the major breadwinner?
- My husband has gone from saying he wants kids someday to not being sure if he ever wants them. I feel betrayed. What can I do to get him to change his mind?

Proviso: *The Complete Marriage Counselor* is not meant as a substitute for therapy. Rather, it is the opening of a dialogue.

And dialogue is essential. The number one complaint I hear is, "My spouse doesn't understand or care about how I feel." Husbands and wives yearn to connect, to feel "gotten." But who couldn't use advice on how to keep that connection vital, nurturing, and alive? On the following pages you get that advice over fifty-fold.

CHAPTER ONE

CHORE WARS

❧

Housework consistently ranks as one of the top argument-provokers among married couples. These disagreements often expose more than the surface dirt festering in a relationship. The spouse who feels he or she is doing the lion's share of chores might feel disrespected, while the one earning the lion's share of the money can feel his or her contributions are not given proper value. And with a recent survey conducted by the Pew Research Center pinpointing that people associate "sharing household chores" as a factor intricately tied to successful marriages, it's crucial that couples get a handle on eliminating if not the mess in the house, then the mess it causes between them.

The experts recruited for this chapter have potentially marriage-saving solutions concerning pivotal issues such as achieving détente between a neat freak and slob and how to create more parity on the housework front when both partners have full-time jobs.

Is it possible for a slob and a neat freak to live together without killing one another?

LeslieBeth Wish, EdD:

Yes. The problem crops up when couples are at extreme frontiers like Felix and Oscar. It's easy to tell a couple to compromise. But what does that mean in concrete, operational terms?

The neat freak has to ask himself or herself, "Of all the areas that make me crazy, where can I let up and slowly begin to build tolerance?" It's helpful to be selective when figuring out which changes to implement. For instance, perhaps you can designate an area in the kitchen where all the shoes and boots can go.

The most important thing is not to enable each other. The neat freak shouldn't chastise, "Oh, how can you stand to live in this pigsty," then clean it. And the slob shouldn't expect his or her partner to do all the cleaning just because that person is very into order.

The partners need to come up with a list of things they're not willing to do. For instance, the wife says, "I won't do your laundry anymore." Her husband will care when he starts running out of clothes. If she's neat and must have everything just so, perhaps she can stop nagging and relax the standards. For instance, every night her husband sits in a chair and cracks walnuts, leaving the shells under the chair. She can hand him a DustBuster and say, "Honey, before we go to sleep can you take care of this?"

Last, lighten up. At any point in a marriage some little thing can lead to an escalation. There's always an opportunity to get whacked out about something your mate does. Pull back for a second and imagine it's you who committed some action that angers your spouse. Would you want him or her to attack you? We all have stupid habits. Make sure you treat your spouse at all times in such a way that he or she still knows you care.

SUSAN HEITLER, PHD:

It's never a good idea to use pejorative terms like "slob" and "neat freak." Get rid of the negative language and use terms that are respectful of one another. Maybe one of you is "casual" about cleanup and the other "likes things organized." This means treating the dilemma as a situation in which "his way" and "her way" leads to "our way."

In a respectful manner, talk over your concerns. One might say, "I don't like picking up after you; I'd prefer if each of us did our own pickup." The more person more oriented to dropping things on the floor might comment, "I'm comfortable with chaos. I've always thrived on clutter."

Just telling your mate, "Clean up your act" won't fly. If he's saying, "Don't be so uptight," that won't fly either. Instead, the one who is more casual can suggest, "How about once a day I make a clean sweep and pick up everything I've dropped around the house?" The other could offer, "What I can do is appreciate your clean sweep rather than criticizing you for things that you dropped during the day." This is part of a turnaround in the relationship—going from criticizing each other, a negative dynamic, to offering solutions and enjoying one another.

To reach the positive, it's often helpful to look at the sources of the "his way" and "her way" mindsets. In one of my cases the husband became much more eager to be responsive to his wife's needs once she explained that her father, who was verbally abusive, went into tirades if she left anything sitting around. The result—anything out of place still brings up in her a panic reaction. The husband explained that in his family everyone's domestic attitude was somewhere between casual and chaotic; there was much laughter and informality. No one worried about messes because the maid came every other day and picked things up. Sharing these stories and seeing the differences in backgrounds, the couple was able to relax, and both of them became more creative and generous with each other about finding solutions.

" MY TAKE "

Both experts contend that many couples routinely fling a lot of dirt at one another when embroiled in a round of the "you're too messy," "well, you're too anal" competition. Dr. Wish and Dr. Heitler exhort couples to realize that beneath their spouse's aggravating sloppy or neatnik exteriors lays a sensitive soul who deserves to be treated with respect and care. At the end of the day, who wouldn't rather cuddle than brood over a dust bunny?

Dr. Wish's suggestion to make a list of chores you will no longer do is a solid one, provided there is follow-through. To threaten to stop doing laundry and then bring out the detergent the first time the hamper overflows undermines your message.

The commitment to follow through is forged through taking Dr. Heitler's advice and sharing the reasons behind your seemingly intransigent issues. Once you can empathize, anger fades, replaced by the desire to work together to find creative solutions.

In the spirit of creativity a couple mired in this situation should try this simple but potent exercise: Spend a day in each other's personas. The neat person should force himself or herself to willy-nilly drop a few papers on the floor and instead of picking them up, throw down a few more. The one who is more comfortable with clutter should in turn become a cleaning machine impassioned to zap dirt no matter how minuscule the speck. At the end of the allotted time for the exercise, come together to debrief. How difficult was it to venture outside the box? And be honest—was there something satisfying about unbending from that usually rigid position? Yes, even clinging to chaos is a rigid position.

Afterward the couple can scurry back to their old habits with the knowledge that it's not the only way to live. Getting a glimpse of how the other half dusts or doesn't dust is another way to bridge the distance and alienation to reach that all-important empathy.

We both have jobs. Why do I have to do all the work around the house?

ELLA LASKY, PhD:

A study of housework trends conducted by the University of Michigan found that a husband creates an extra seven hours a week of housework for his partner. On the other hand, having a wife saves men from about an hour of housework a week. The load increases dramatically when children are involved.

The husband probably has a different perception than his wife about how much he does around the house. He may do more than his dad did, but not as much as his wife wishes. I would encourage couples to outline exactly what chores each performs. Perhaps she doesn't notice how long it takes him to pick up leaves from the yard. Maybe he doesn't realize how often she does basic tasks like laundry and buying milk. The point is to move from a blaming situation where she says he doesn't do anything to each seeing what the other actually does and then collaborating on shifting things around.

Next the couple should ask the question, "Is everything we're doing necessary?" Perhaps one is more of a perfectionist; for example, washing an item even if it's only been worn once. Not everything has to immediately be thrown in the washing machine. Or maybe some of the tasks don't need to be done at all, such as preparing full-course meals nightly.

A useful technique is to make a list of recurring household tasks. Each partner then decides which tasks he or she is willing to do and which he or she really hates. Ideally each takes on a task that displeases the other. Then they divvy up the rest. This schedule is followed for a week, a month, whatever is decided. Then the couple checks back to see how it's working out, and makes readjustments as needed.

For husbands who don't understand why their spouse feels the division of labor is unfair, I ask them, "Is it fair that your wife comes home from work and while you're relaxing she's putting in X amount of hours working? Shouldn't you both have time to relax?" If a man says, "No, she's the woman. That's what she's supposed to do," then I say, "She's not going to have much energy left over for you." I try to work through each of his objections, maintaining curiosity about which parts of the arrangement are working and which aren't, and not being judgmental.

The wife won't get far by merely venting. She has to step back and have a respectful conversation, being descriptive, not judgmental: "Okay, John. You want me to do all this and when I do it makes me feel such and such." She is stating how she feels but not blaming her husband.

The resentment she feels often feeds into her being too tired to have sex. That will get her husband's attention!

Kathryn Janus:

This is an issue for 75 percent of couples. Let's say he leaves his socks on the floor or his glass on the table. The wife interprets this behavior as disrespectful and feels taken for granted. Over time her anger builds until it becomes rage. This turns into her nagging her mate. The result—he does less instead of more, especially if her actions trigger memories of being raised by an invasive mother. If this dynamic continues between the couple—the wife nagging, her husband retreating—her chronic anger will lead to her shutting down sexually.

The truth, however, is that rarely is the husband being disrespectful or taking his wife for granted. The chore disparity is about a difference in perception. The messy partner truly doesn't see his mess as mess. The towel hanging on the door doesn't bother him. The solution is for couples to discuss the impasse calmly. The wife must express how deeply hurt she is by the man's behavior. The husband in turn needs to assert he means no disrespect.

I tell a male client he should view pitching in as foreplay. If he willingly helps out around the house it will lead to a happier relationship. If he remains completely disinterested in chores, the couple must find money for a housekeeper. If this option is impossible, I suggest the wife make a list of all household chores. "I need more help around the house" is vague. She must show her spouse exactly what she wants him to do. He is not a mind reader. Direction is needed. And—here's where it gets dicey—she must let go of having the chore done exactly the way she wishes. Instead, the wife should relinquish control; let him do the task as he sees fit, then thank him for his effort.

" MY TAKE "

The experts do their best to clean up the mess caused by fights centered on housework disparities. Dr. Lasky's suggestion that the couple detail exactly what each does to keep the joint humming is a sound one. The majority of husbands may not do as much as their mate, but they also rarely receive as much credit for tasks they do perform. I also like the therapist's suggestion about divvying up chores, each leaving to the other the most hated tasks. A potential wrinkle here is that if each spouse were willing to commit to taking on regular tasks in the first place, they wouldn't be fighting.

Janus's main point is a perceptive one. What's merely a glass sitting on a table to one person is a symbol of chaos to the other. This glaring difference in discernment means the couple needs to communicate their feelings, viewpoints, and desires clearly and sans rancor. Her suggestion to lessen the standards by which said tasks are performed may be tough in the short term, but over the long haul could be a sanity saver.

Both experts are of the animal trainer mode—promise the husband a treat (i.e., the prospect of sex) and he'll heel and fetch on command.

Spinning off Dr. Lasky's suggestion of telling a spouse which chores feel only slightly less enjoyable than dental surgery, the reverse strategy can be helpful as well. Ask what jobs hold most appeal. He's a budding chef? Let him take over more of the shopping, cooking, and meal planning. And take a time-out. Stop holding marathon housework sessions over the weekend. Instead, spread mopping, sweeping, and dusting detail over the week. Maybe Wednesday could be laundry night. That way a chore-free Saturday is possible.

While we're on the subject of time-outs, a couple should take one together. Put the tension over housework on hold (worry not; it won't go away) and put energy into reconnecting. Revisit the scene of the storied first date. Take a walk hand in hand on the beach. Laugh together. When a return is made to the bargaining table the couple will be more in the spirit of détente than standoff.

Why does he want a medal for taking out the trash?

Scott Haltzman, MD:

When a man returns from war he expects his wife to hurl herself into his arms and give him a kiss. Inwardly all guys want to be heroes and rewarded when they do something small. This sounds silly to women. They tell me, "I don't need to be thanked every time I fold a shirt!"

That's just how men are. Not automatically remembering to do a household chore isn't meant as a slight to you. Their intention is good but the task isn't stored in their memory. In fact, studies show men feel underappreciated for tasks they do—like fixing broken chairs, yard work. . . .

In a just world a man would take out the trash without prompting. In our non-just world, a wife must use positive reinforcement. Say, "I'll be in bed waiting after you empty the dishwasher." Or try humor: Get him a T-shirt emblazoned with "I'm the guy who takes the trash out." Or prompt him: Schedule his cell phone so it beeps around the time the trash needs taking out. A great way to prod him into action is to do it yourself. If I see my wife pulling the trash bag out from under the sink, I'll say, "What are you doing? That's my job." Or if you time it well, he'll be pulling into the driveway just as you're dragging a heavy garbage can to the curb for pickup the next morning. This will trigger his hero instinct and he'll pull over and perform a "rescue."

The bottom line: You can either get angry about his forgetfulness or roll with it. And that's not trash talk.

WARREN FARRELL, PhD:

What he's thinking is that he'll never get a medal or even recognition for all the contributions that he makes. Arlie Russell Hochschild's housework study documented in *The Second Shift* didn't include tasks done as needed, such as researching online which new computer to buy, double-checking the price at Radio Shack, and buying and hooking it up; remodeling the kids' room; dealing with a roof leak; and shoveling snow.

He doesn't keep track or discuss the chores he routinely performs. Men know that in the home the woman has control. Wives can't hear what husbands can't say. When I told a group of married men that I write books on male and female relationships one of them laughed and said: "Oh, you mean 'Say yes or die.'" His friends laughed in agreement.

Statistically when a woman is the major breadwinner her husband will do the bulk of the housework and childcare. This is not true if the woman works more hours but makes a lower salary. A man views the job of supporting the household as a responsibility, a burden. In his eyes it's a forfeiting, not a flexing of power to have employment that causes him to give up free time to do things he'd enjoy more, such as relaxing with his family, exercising, or being with friends. If he's the primary breadwinner he's thinking on some level but would never have the guts to tell his wife, "I don't ask you to come to my workplace and pitch in. Why should I go to yours?"

Still, if a woman shows by her tone and body language that she's grateful when he takes out the trash, he'll do it. All a man wants is to be acknowledged and appreciated. Then he might even do the chore without being asked. But if the request is made in a long-suffering tone, odds are the wife will continue to suffer.

" MY TAKE "

Dr. Haltzman and Dr. Farrell both sound the trumpet call to appreciate the household contributions of one's mate no matter how ill-justified uttering such thanks for performing mundane chores may seem. This may appear illogical given that men's style of communication is typically predicated on logical versus emotional reasoning. They can't understand why their wives need so much reassurance and praise: "Of course you look thin in those jeans, honey!"

Women are bewildered and pained by men's more distant way of relating. They wish their men would share every thought, take every opportunity to compliment their wives on their accomplishments, both bring romance to the table and wipe off the crumbs. Yet the experts state that the need of these logical creatures to please the women in their lives is so enormous it makes them ripe for manipulation.

The advice here is to give the lug what he craves in order to get what you perceive he should be doing automatically. This point is valid, though I'm a little wary of Dr. Haltzman's "empty the dishwasher and I'll make your toes curl" pandering unless you're really in the mood to make his toes curl. Making sex—indeed doing any favor for your mate a quid pro quo—sets a false and sad foundation for a loving, caring, mature marriage.

The look into the crevices of the male mind is an invaluable aid in the sometimes uphill and always essential task of understanding the opposite sex. A wife might passionately believe that a husband doesn't pull his weight when it comes to keeping the house running smoothly. He harbors an equally passionate belief that not only does he do his fair share, his wife has no appreciation for his manly labors. The likelihood is that neither is 100 percent right nor 100 percent wrong. However, a wife refusing to acknowledge her husband's right to feel differently is a double-fault—he feels invalidated and she still has to lug out the trash.

If it's difficult to wrap one's mouth around the word "thanks" when the recipient is a spouse, pretend the expression of gratitude is being voiced to a stranger or acquaintance. It's a human tendency to treat one's nearest and dearest the most carelessly. View a mate as a person, not a pet that is constantly soiling the carpet.

Bestow thanks grudgingly and the sarcasm and/or secret derision will be noticed. To help muster sincere gratitude, think about his contributions. Few wives want to venture onto the roof to repair a leak.

Thank him for doing something small; he'll keep doing it and perhaps move on to larger things. Today the trash, tomorrow toilet scrubbing!

FIELD REPORT

I have been married to my college sweetheart for fifteen years. We used to fight about stupid stuff like housework, but at the bottom of those issues were things like, "I don't get to spend enough time with you, and when you are home, I don't feel like I am a priority." This is how the trash or laundry becomes a deal-breaking issue with people—they think they are talking about taking out the garbage, but they are really talking about being afraid of the future, about security, about getting their needs met. Once we realized most of our fights could be dealt with if we concentrated on trying to solve the problem, not magically fix our fatally flawed and imperfect partner, and realized that many times our fights were more about "Miss you" than "You are inconsiderate," life became much, much better.

~Whitney Hoffman, 45, Chadds Ford, Pennsylvania

CHAPTER TWO

MONEY FIGHTS CAN BANKRUPT YOUR RELATIONSHIP

It has been said (often and loudly) that money is the number one thing couples fight about. Money hits at the core of who we are. Our money personalities are formed early and often lead to couples having conflicting spending and saving styles and incessant power struggles as they cling to outdated perceptions of what money roles should be in a relationship. The tribulations tackled by the team of top-tier marriage experts assembled for this chapter include issues that arise when the couple is in debt, the wife is the major breadwinner, or the couple experiences what Freud phrased "the last taboo"—being unable to talk about money, even with the person with whom one shares both a bed and bank statement!

How can we keep the pressure of being in debt from crushing our relationship?

SUSAN HEITLER, PhD:

First identify a specific element of your situation that has been divisive. Then look at what your response has been. For instance, is one of you blaming the other for debts? Perhaps one of you made an investment or a large purchase that caused the debt. Turn lemons into lemonade by moving from combative, backwards-looking, "whose fault is it" arguing to collaborative, forward-looking problem solving.

How can you solve problems collaboratively when one of you wants Plan X and the other Plan Y? Switch from arguing about who's going to be the winner to looking at the underlying concerns, and then find a solution responsive to both of your concerns. For instance, say your spouse wants a new car and you don't want to spend so much money. Share your concerns. He might feel it's important for his career that he look established, while you don't want to go further into debt. A win-win solution might be to lease a car.

Is worrying making it hard for you to handle being in debt? Then the task becomes how to move from worrying to problem solving. If you're worried the two of you won't be able to pay the mortgage, face that fear squarely, and again, figure out a plan of action. Maybe as much as you love your house you may need to sell it and rent for the next two years.

In sum, avoid pointing the finger of blame or dissolving in a whirl of worries. Instead, remember that problems are for solving. And above all, especially in hard economic times, remember that at least you have each other. Loving is free. Give lots.

OLIVIA MELLAN:

It's necessary to establish a climate of safety and trust.

Find a time when neither of you feels stressed, and the kids aren't around, to practice empathetic communication. This is done by doing active listening—mirroring, validating, and empathizing. Start by saying something nice to each other, one quick sentence: "I appreciate that you made me breakfast this morning" or "I appreciate that you do so many errands."

Then take turns speaking about your concerns. For example, the wife says, "I am worried about money." The husband mirrors, "I hear that you are worried about money." The couple goes back and forth until all of the wife's worries are voiced. Then the husband validates, "It makes sense you are nervous about the debt because. . . ." There is no attacking. Then it is the husband's turn to voice his worries and to feel fully heard and validated.

Once you are empathetic with one another it becomes easier to create a plan together to get out of debt. Both of you should keep what I call an Emotional Spending Diary. Each person writes down every penny spent during the week and how he or she felt at the time of the purchase. For example, "I was bored when I bought this. It was a waste." At the end of the week put the purchases into categories. Identify the places you get into trouble. See where you can tweak things to create a "spending plan," a term I like better than "budget." If you're totally into electronic equipment, are you buying things you don't need? Where there is debt there is usually a spender. How judgmental is the non-spender? Again it comes back to the empathetic communication and not attacking.

The two of you should also compose a list of money goals. Separately write down short-term, medium-term, and long-term goals after agreeing on what exactly those terms mean. Many of those goals will involve money: I want to get out of debt; I want to redecorate; I want to send the kids to college. You should compare the lists, then redo them several times to see which goals emerge as most important for both of you.

Have weekly money meetings where you sit down, go over the goals, and look at the bills. Where can you cut back? Working together, you can get through this difficult time.

" MY TAKE "

The money message here is to take care of the feelings before the finances. When you're busy fighting each other—blaming, withholding, and so on—there's no energy left to devote to whittling down the debt. Mellan's suggestion of empathetic communication is sound, although this strategy can be difficult to implement in the best of times without a trained professional "cheerleading" you. Obviously, with the pressure of debt, the present is not the best of times. Make a sincere effort to listen to one another's point of view, taking a deep breath (biting your tongue if necessary) to keep yourself from attacking, blaming, and/or acting defensive. To stay on track, keep in mind that how you got into debt is not the most important factor at this point; what matters is forging a common goal of getting out of the hole. The more you can make this a "you and me against the world" dilemma versus "you against me," the more your relationship will benefit.

Mellan's Emotional Spending Diary is a helpful tool, as is Dr. Heitler's plan to trade in the boxing gloves for a stroll down the collaboration zone.

Debt management for couples is tricky business. Perilous business. In 2005, according to *www.cardweb.com*, households with at least one credit card carried $9,498 in card debt—a 50 percent increase over the previous decade. As the experts' sage advice has demonstrated, it is tough for couples to work collaboratively on their wayward finances. Thus it makes sense to seek the services of a local debt counselor. Make sure the debt consolidation credit counseling agency is reputable by checking whether it is endorsed by the Council on Accreditation of Services for Families and Children, Inc. (COA).

Why does she always give me a hard time about what I buy?

JAY P. GRANAT, PHD:

I'm a believer in trying the simplest solution first. Part of this solution can be a review of finances leading to an agreement: "Okay, if there's a purchase I want to make that's above X amount of dollars I'll discuss it with you first. Under that amount I can buy anything I want."

Occasionally the couple's money-managing disputes are in a vacuum. They are otherwise a good team and can look at this problem as a bump in the road. Frequently, though, there is a lot of resentment and hurt simmering over many issues, not just money. For example, does this pair have trouble trusting each other?

It can be helpful for the couple to explore their attitudes and insecurities about money. If one person is overspending, is perhaps even a shopping addict, it could be related to an underlying depression. Medication and ongoing therapy might be required so that he or she can recognize self-defeating behaviors. Often someone who overspends does so in an attempt to fill the psychological emptiness with objects. Of course this doesn't work over the long term.

Another reason someone might continually make purchases that will annoy his or her spouse is to feel a sense of control. Thus commences the power struggle. In a relationship there should be two executive officers, a co-CEO model. If the couple can realign things and develop a plan around spending money that feels comfortable for both, their prognosis improves.

CHRISTINE MORIARTY, CFP:

My guess is the one giving the worst time to the other is the one primarily in charge of finances. Blame it on a need for control and/or communication issues. He or she could be a control freak and thus wants to authorize all the expenditures. Or one spouse had something in mind for that money but never communicated those plans and now finds out those funds were spent.

In terms of communication, couples need to discuss financial priorities—where money should go, what purchases they need as a family, etc. For instance, a man doesn't typically feel decorating a house is important. But his wife does. Or the wife is angry her spouse bought the most expensive camera on the market. It might not be the expense itself that's upsetting, but that she wasn't consulted. This is something both partners need to work on—making financial desires known.

Control problems can be tougher to resolve but are still workable. Perhaps the wife is the one who doesn't have much say in where money goes. She needs to start doing things, such as balancing the checkbook, so her husband can trust her with these tasks. Say she spent a lot of money on an item because she was unaware there wasn't enough in the account to cover it. The husband's anger might be about feeling inadequate, that he wasn't able to properly provide for his family. Of course in some families it's the wife who controls where the money goes. But both partners need to look at the dynamic at play and work to change it.

" MY TAKE "

Dr. Granat's suggestion that the couple set a figure above which they cannot spend without a prior conversation can be an exemplary fight-buster, an instance of problem solving at its finest. The proviso is the pair must be able to disentangle themselves from those murky motives and dank emotions that are often causative factors behind a financial dispute. It's difficult to be rational about money but so rewarding if that objective is achieved.

Both experts allude to the push for power as a frequent factor in money fights. I particularly like Moriarty's assertion that the one most incensed by unapproved purchases is the spouse who commonly has a stranglehold on the household purse strings. However, while the expert gives lip service to the idea that the woman might be the primary financial decider, Moriarty clearly feels that monetarily speaking, it remains primarily a man's world.

Financial aspirations can bring a couple together rather than pull them apart. Set money goals toward purchases that will bring mutual satisfaction; for example, a vacation. The larger the goal—toward a down payment on a house—the more connected the pair will feel.

Why is it so tough to talk about money with each other?

BARTON GOLDSMITH, PhD:

Money is the number one cause of divorce. It connects to issues about power and freedom. It's primal—not surprising since money is tied to our very survival. Thus it makes us angry, scared and possessive: I should be able to do what I want with my money!

Yet many couples don't talk about money at all. Or if they do, it's without sufficiently understanding the root of their partner's financial personality. How your families dealt with money has a lot to do with your financial style. A saver may feel anxiety when there aren't a few bucks in the bank while a spender thinks, "I can easily afford this flat-screen TV. I'm getting a check next week."

Getting to the core beliefs helps you go beyond thinking your spouse is a skinflint and into realizing, "He was raised never knowing when his spendthrift dad was going to blow a week's pay on booze. No wonder he's insecure." The important thing with money discussions is to be open and honest. For instance, confess if you've run up credit card debt. Keep in mind that hiding money is like infidelity—it will leave deep wounds.

Lean toward balance, not control. If one of you is the primary breadwinner, don't make your loved one feel like he or she has to come begging for money. Somewhere in the sixties the word "obey" was removed from the marriage vows. The word "compromise" should replace it. It's not just you and your partner in the marriage;

there's a third entity—us. Say the spender in the family wants to use a windfall to remodel the house. The saver wants to bank the money. A compromise can be banking enough to allay most of the saver's fears and then spending the rest, which pleases the partner who believes having money allows for freedom and self-expression.

JOHN CURTIS, PhD:

It's said that money is the number one cause of divorce, but really money issues are connected to many other factors. Think of an octopus with all those tentacles. Generational and gender differences can impact the ways one or both view money. Regardless, it's always a challenging, sensitive issue to discuss. A woman once said the male ego was her partner's second-most delicate organ. And the ego certainly gets a rise around what money means in a marriage, especially when one partner is swinging it around as a weapon.

Conflicts about money are really conflicts about values. Say the wife wants to give the church 10 percent of every dollar the couple makes; the husband is agnostic and doesn't want to make any donations. The underlying battle is about religious belief systems. Can there be a compromise? Perhaps, perhaps not, depending on the rigidity of the positions.

" MY TAKE "

Debating whether money is or isn't the number one cause of divorce sidetracks us from the indisputable truth that couples are married not just to one another, but to the spouse's often contrary views on money. Possible red flags ahead. Happily, a side-by-side look at both experts' perspectives brings a multilayered perspective to this problem.

Dr. Goldsmith's assertion that a person's views on money are informed by dynamics in the family into which one was born is dead-on. Understanding why one's partner holds such an obstinate and frustrating position on all matters of the purse strings can help promote empathy rather than another round of, "Why are you so weird about money? I can't deal with you!"

Money is not a fun or sexy topic but as Dr. Goldsmith says, unless financial differences are aired in an open, honest way with compromise the end goal, a couple might wind up hiring divorce lawyers. Those don't come cheap!

Dr. Curtis's observation that while conflicts might appear straight-forwardly money-centric, they are woven into disputes over differing value systems. Until there is clarity about what it is that truly makes a couple hold sometimes intransigent beliefs, it is impossible to really get a handle on what is needed to bridge the gulf between the pair.

It is crucial to be financially generous toward one's spouse. It's not necessary to encourage a partner's craving for Manolo Blahnik shoes and Prada bags, unless she can easily afford it. However, recognize that it is important for her to dress in a way that makes her feel beautiful and special. The same principle applies to a partner wanting pricey tickets for every home game featuring his favorite sports team. Perhaps such extravagance isn't fiscally feasible. Then the wife can gently steer her husband toward the nosebleed section, but for a special occasion surprise him with seats so close they're practically sitting on the team bench.

It's equally important to guard against being emotionally stingy. Notice when a spouse's favorite group puts out a new CD and download it for her. Call and ask how her job interview went. Don't share a partner's adoration for all things Disney? That's your prerogative, but don't make fun of the Mouse.

How can I handle my wife being the major breadwinner?

DON AND MARTHA ROSENTHAL:

This question is posed by someone coming from a place of social conditioning that implies there is something wrong if the wife is the major breadwinner.

The question should be, "Are my wife and I both contributing as equals in the marriage, the contribution not based solely on
who is making more money?" A second question should be, "Are we
spending our days doing things that reflect who we really are, things
that nourish our souls, not just our pocketbooks?" If that's the case,
these people are fortunate.

More important than the flow of love is that there be a balance in the relationship in the form of what each partner contrib-
utes. Perhaps the man gets to develop his latent feminine nature by
spending time at home with the kids while the wife explores her
latent masculinity by being out in the world. If he can get beyond
his traditional masculine pride that dictates he should earn the
majority of the household income, this situation can bless both of
them.

What is really important is that both people spend their
days involved in activities that feel fulfilling, and that the couple
experience a sense of balance in the relationship. This outcome
is a product of which is stronger—resentment or love. When it
tips over to the latter the husband is thinking, "It would be fine
if I earned a living and Martha didn't earn any money or vice
versa."

Marriage involves shopping, paying bills, taking care of children. . . . In a partnership where there is love, there is a great deal of
flexibility. The balance can shift over time. He can earn more money,
then it can shift—and it's all fine.

OLIVIA MELLAN:

When I look at a couple with this issue I look at the qualities each
brings to the relationship. Some people are good at nurturing, some
at handling money, some excel academically, and so on.

Right now this husband sees himself solely in the role he's
supposed to be playing—major breadwinner. Is he less of a man
if he isn't accomplishing this goal? How else can he find value
in himself? What does he think his wife finds of value in him?

Does he feel undermined if he's not living up to his expectations of himself?

Where did these expectations come from? How was he raised? What was a man supposed to be? If he didn't meet that role, what would it mean? Does he now feel ashamed, sad that he can't meet what he perceives as his obligations? And in the wife's eyes, what does it mean to be a woman? Is she comfortable earning more than her husband? This may look like the man's issue, but each needs to look at the feelings her higher income dredges up in order to find clarity.

This involves them looking at the values each brings to the relationship. The husband needs to see what he brings to the table in all aspects, not just monetarily. To accomplish this he should ask his wife what attracted her to him. Getting this information can help him understand there is a lot more to him than his wallet. He also needs to remind himself of what he finds attractive in her. Doubtless it's a lot more than her moneymaking ability. He should then share these insights with her.

If the two of them can talk about these matters, they begin forming a more realistic union. They will have a more genuine view of each other rather than one based on the expectations of what a man and woman are supposed to do.

" MY TAKE "

There is much of value here that goes well beyond the monetary kind. The Rosenthals and Mellan strongly agree that people have to discover and come to accept who they are as individuals, not just robotically assume a socially dictated role. Each expert makes some unique points as well.

According to the Rosenthals, love is not the answer. While that special feeling is extremely important, the husband-and-wife thera- pist team maintain that the true key to marital happiness is balance. This involves men and women cueing into their dormant feminine and masculine natures. Loving each other isn't enough—and love doesn't mean you shouldn't say you're sorry! A couple's roles in a marriage should be fluid and not fixed by sexist and separatist ideology. But here's a nitpicky point. The most crucial element of a successful union is that both partners are committed to stick it out regardless of the inevitable ebbs and flows. If one or both have the attitude that "I'm here until it gets tough," the relationship will be strained by a crisis, and the fallout can be divorce.

I love Mellan's suggestion that the couple voice what they find special about one another. Too often partners assume the other knows why he or she is loved; no extra effort need be made. That assumption is often wrong. It's essential on a regular basis to make one another feel cared about. In that kind of supportive environment partners will feel truly able to share their deepest fears and insecurities when something occurs that causes a tremendous drop in self-esteem.

That drop in self-esteem is due to the husband's internal life being ruled by external factors. He can only feel good about himself if there are things going on in his life that will impress others, including his wife. If he can get to a place of less ego where the world doesn't revolve around celebrating me, me, me, he will truly be able to celebrate his partner's successes rather than being stuck in how those successes impact him.

Learning to handle and even thrive in times when the wife is more outwardly successful is not a luxury but an imperative when you consider that the 2004 census found that in one-fourth of dual-earner families, wives outearned their husbands, up from one-sixth of two-income families in 1981.

Why does he make all the financial decisions?

Christine Moriarty, CFP:

The short answer: Because she lets him. Money is power, and men tend to be more verbally powerful. However, it's seldom that simple. Women actually spend more of the household money on a daily basis on food, clothes for the children, and the like. Indeed, wives tend to make all the decisions around children—everything from how many the couple has to what schools they go to. So it might appear the husband makes all the major decisions, but the wife is often the driver.

Is the agreement the wife now abhors one that was consciously discussed early in their marriage, or did it evolve on a subconscious level? Does the couple operate as a team in other ways, or does each often seem to be in his or her own sphere of influence? Does he make random financial decisions, say buying a home computer or deciding on a vacation spot, without first having discussions with his wife?

If that's the case, the couple should start from scratch and rebuild the financial pieces. They need money designated as his, hers, ours. The specifics of this arrangement would be each person having little pools of money to spend as desired, anywhere from $100 to $1,000 a month depending on their circumstances. Then there is money that is earmarked to be spent only after mutual discussion.

The wife needs to know where everything is—401(k) investments, stocks, and so on. She should say, "We need to take more of an attitude of joint responsibility. You don't have to shoulder everything." Perhaps they should see a financial adviser to help them work things out.

PHIL KIRSCHBAUM, LCSW:

What I often find is this was an agreement the couple made earlier in the relationship. Now the wife has done some growing and is no longer okay with being totally dependent on her husband. It constitutes her desire for a shift toward interdependency. Not every guy is ready to do that. It can spell disaster when one spouse is growing and the other isn't.

However, the husband can also negotiate some of what he wants in this shift. Maybe there's something he'd like to see changed.

It then becomes a rebalancing, a quid pro quo: You give me some of this I've been wanting, and I'll give you the thing you want. When viewed in this way the wife's desires can be viewed not as a threat but a stepping stone for the husband.

A dialogue needs to occur around money and expenses. The couple can develop a budget that is mutually arrived at. This is an intimate act and helps negate the fear the husband might feel about just handing over the checkbook. Sometimes a counselor needs to be a third party to help the couple negotiate this new agreement. Again, the new order isn't a switch from the husband being in charge to being dependent on the wife, but about the two of them working out a plan that either one can implement vis-à-vis where money goes.

Creating a budget involves going over everything line by line. What are the fixed expenses, the discretionary funds? Can they arrive at a figure each can support in terms of saving for the kids' education, making large purchases, entertainment. . . ? Often a couple has different ideas of how much to spend and how much to save. The process of working this out in a fair way can be intense. For the wife right now it's a mystery how the finances are being managed. Sometimes there's a power in keeping the other person in the dark, but often it's not so much about wanting control as maintaining the status quo: You said you were lousy with money and you wanted me to take care of it. But that was five, ten, fifteen years ago. The wife is no longer the same person, and the husband hopefully can become acclimated to this.

" MY TAKE "

I love Moriarty's pithy answer: Because she lets him. It's a good reminder that we are not bystanders to our lives. Rather we have control, even if the way we exercise that control is by ceding it. Along the same lines, I like her suggestion that the wife might have more power around decision-making than she realizes.

Kirschbaum's insight that the wife's best strategy is to show the husband she's looking for negotiation, and not a hostile takeover in the decision-making department, is on the money. The husband needs to feel there is something in this new order for him or he will be extremely resistant to the idea of change. And of course, as the expert points out, the change should be grounded in something concrete, not ephemeral—an actual budget.

According to the National Center for Women and Retirement Research, 80 percent to 90 percent of women will be responsible for their finances at some point. More depressing facts: Studies conducted by AARP show that three out of five women earn under $30,000 annually. At age sixty-five and older, 40 percent of women live alone, compared to 19 percent of men.

What all of this means, obviously, is that it's not muscle-flexing for a woman to want more financial knowledge and power; it's a necessity. If a husband suddenly leaves or dies and his wife has no clue where the financial records are, or if the couple is in debt, a tough, traumatic situation concurrently becomes a full-fledged crisis. If a wife approaches her husband with these facts, it may mitigate any potential antagonism.

FIELD REPORT

Probably the worst irritant is our finances, so we have learned to face it jointly instead of pit ourselves against each other. Meaning when discussing money issues, we consciously sit on the same side of the table and address the problem together, out in front of us, as opposed to sitting on opposite ends and having a debate. Sitting side by side is a reminder that it is "us" attacking the problem, not us attacking each other.

~Mary C. Trefney, 45, Whitmore Lake, Michigan

LASTING LOVE

Sharon and John Dotson
Houston, Texas; married twenty-six years

"The marriage is imperfect sometimes but we'd never abandon it."

This couple's story epitomizes the maxim that if at first you don't succeed, try again.

When they met on Halloween 1982 at a singles function at their local church, John was forty-seven and Sharon thirty-seven. Between them they had six children from long and difficult marriages. Yet within five months they married.

John says, "We were conservative people who did a very nonconservative thing."

Alas, this wildly impulsive romantic leap of faith didn't immediately result in the mythical happily after ever with icing and cherries on top. There was a run of hard times—for a brief scary patch, both were simultaneously unemployed with $2,000 between them; John was struck with testicular cancer; and one of Sharon's sons has Asperger's syndrome.

How did they handle these trials? "Everyone has struggles," Sharon explains, adding, "We barely knew each other when we married, but our values were and are the same."

John elaborates, "We go in the same direction."

Words tumble out from Sharon. "In my previous marriage I'd want something one way, my husband another." John adds, "Problems are something to solve together, not blame each other for."

Sharon's voice exudes gratitude as she proclaims, "It's not like we haven't had hundreds of arguments over the years, but I've never believed John had anything but my best interests at heart."

Laughing, she confides, "One time after a fight he got in the car and drove away." The kicker: "I knew he'd come back. He had no clothes."

The couple's worst stressor was ongoing for the first seven years of their marriage. John's children—"fed a line of propaganda by their mother"—cut him out of their lives to the point that he wasn't told where they lived. "Every time I thought of them I cried until I couldn't cry anymore!"

One miraculous day, after reservoirs of tears, the phone rang. It was his youngest daughter. She'd had a premonition her father was in trouble. Indeed, he'd just come out of the hospital after surgery for the cancer. He is now in contact with all his children. "No one's forgotten. It still hurts, but we've put the trouble in the past."

The marriage hasn't all been about surmounting turmoil; there has been much joy and mutual satisfaction. Together the couple bought a home, raised an unwieldy brood, and forged successful careers—he's an attorney; she runs a public relations firm.

"We haven't had a Norman Rockwell Americana kind of life," says John. "Our two sets of children are rarely in the same room together, though we've tried to make that happen."

Sharon adds, "The divorce rate for remarriages is higher than for first ones." She is silent, pondering, then adds a final assessment of her "together forever" union: "I wouldn't advise anyone to marry after five months, but I was very much in love. Many obstacles have been put in our path, but John and I managed to climb over them together."

CHAPTER THREE

CAN THIS SEX LIFE
BE SAVED?

❧

While great sex does not ensure a great relationship, unsatisfying sex can be a majority contributor to the deadly troika of marital pitfalls: hostility, indifference, and infidelity. Couples who devote time and energy to creating and maintaining a healthy sex life tend to be more connected and suffer less from health problems.

This chapter utilizes input from marriage counselors who specialize in matters of the boudoir. The questions here address a host of sexual issues that can befall couples—ranging from boredom and monotony to fearing one's partner has lost that lusting feeling to exploring some men's penchant for porn to wondering if monogamy is a passé concept. Enough foreplay. Dip in.

My wife and I have been together five years and sex is getting boring. How can I get her interested in trying new things in bed?

MARY HAMMOND, MA:

My first question is, "What is the husband's motivation?" His wish won't materialize if he's coming from a self-centered place. It should be about, "What can I give?" as well as, "What can I get?" He needs to ask his wife what she wants as well; what pleasures her? Hopefully they will have an exchange about what each wants, and meet in the middle.

Many couples in their thirties and forties have a distorted view of sexuality. For instance, they shouldn't buy in to how often they should have sex as depicted by the media. Happy couples have sex more frequently than unhappy ones. But each spouse has to ask how often would be optimal and then see how close or far apart that is from the other person's desire.

Another piece is that in the old tradition sex was part of a spiritual path. It's not often thought of in that way anymore. So if couples can begin to think of sex as not only fun but a part of love and an expression of spirituality, it can take them to a deeper place.

Also, one spouse, typically the man, is more attracted to the visual while the other needs more emotional connection in order to get turned on. So as couples work together on their emotional life, it deepens the sexual experience. Men find they enjoy experiencing sex on more than a surface level.

This husband should keep asking his wife, "What can I do to make you feel safe?" In this context he wouldn't push for trying new things more frequently than his wife can handle. Say something new is tried two or three times a month rather than two or three times a week. The couple needs to discuss when they want sex to be romantic and loving and when it should be playful. Those can be different experiences, fulfilling on different levels.

JOYCE MORLEY-BALL, EdD:

The wife's initial reaction is probably, "How did you hear about this kind of move? Where does it come from?" It's important to be clear it came from a book or film: "I've never tried it but I'd like us to do it together."

Then the husband has to get her interested. He wants his wife to try something new and different. Dealing with change is difficult, so there has to be confidence and trust on her part. Also, he has to guide her through exactly what he wants her to do differently . . . and to point out that what matters isn't just what he gets out of it, but also what feels good for her.

Maybe he can show her what the benefits would be, gently touching her, showing her how much he loves her, making sure they're on the same page. Hopefully all this will help allay some of her concerns. But he needs to be patient. It might not happen that day. He might broach the subject another time. Rather than inducing a guilt trip or placing blame—"You never do anything for me"—he can use "I" messages: "Remember what I talked about before? Is that something we can explore? It would mean the world to me." Let her know he is willing to be patient, but will revisit the topic from time to time.

Last, he should offer his wife the option to suggest something different as well.

" MY TAKE "

If you get nothing else from the sound advice here, mark Dr. Morley-Ball's savvy comment that the first reaction on the wife's part will likely be suspicion. Unless change is one's own idea, the reaction might be discomfort. People cover up discomfort by attacking. The marriage expert also rightly suggests that the husband has to show the wife that the addition to their sexual repertoire will make her a happy girl.

Hammond fervently agrees that attention must be paid to the wife's pleasure, though she perhaps goes a teensy bit overboard on the "make it feel safe for the woman" part, unless the wife is damaged in some way from past abuse and/or the husband is jonesing for something that the wife finds disrespectful. After all, this couple has been together five years, thus supposedly around the rink a time or ten. However, I applaud the therapist's point that many in our society have a distorted view of sexuality. People need to look at what makes them happy versus what the media portrays as "normal."

It is of paramount importance for the husband not to put the wife on the defensive or make her feel insecure, boring, and/or untalented in the boudoir.

Timing is important. Here's a good rule of thumb: Don't initiate a talk about one's sexual dissatisfaction while physically engaged. Bring up the topic casually, perhaps during a quiet evening at home. Use words that are ego-enhancing rather than ego-wounding. The husband should begin with compliments: "You're as beautiful and attractive to me as ever. I love how you really know my body and what feels good to me."

THE MORAL: Positive psychological strokes can lead to positive physical ones.

Can monogamy work?

Esther Perel:

The meaning of monogamy, like the meaning of marriage, sex, and intimacy, has changed drastically in the past century. Historically, monogamy was a mainstay of patriarchy, meant to ascertain patrimony and lineage. It was imposed on women, and a general double standard prevailed. It had nothing to do with love. Today it has everything to do with love. From an imposition it has become a conviction espoused in the West by both genders, a unique marker of our specialness.

Monogamy became the sacred cow of the romantic ideal. Parallel to our ongoing concern with privacy and boundaries, the proliferation of infidelity travels alongside the enduring ideal of monogamy. It is important to keep sight of these complexities, and to address the issues nonjudgmentally, with nuance and multicultural perspective. My purpose is to create a therapeutic environment where people can discuss their longings, frustrations, and hopes with an aim toward moving the relationship forward whether it is monogamous or not. Chief in the conversation is the extent to which monogamy is bound by notions of sexual exclusivity. Some people prefer to stress emotional commitment, loyalty, and primacy of the relationship as the central elements of monogamy at the expense of sexual exclusivity. It seems that many people remain sexually faithful yet emotionally betray each other in a variety of ways, while others prefer to be emotionally faithful and sexually diverse. It is not for me to impose a definition of monogamy.

Couples today are better served by negotiating the boundaries rather than tacitly assuming both partners share similar definitions. Many people hold the value of monogamy, and then find there is a gap between their values and their behavior.

When does a relationship start to be non-monogamous? When someone fantasizes about others? When someone looks at others? What does non-monogamy mean? Flirting? Having friendships with people of the opposite sex? This is a moving target. Wherever people draw their demarcation, what lies outside is seen as unfaithful. While for some the definitions are tight, for others there is great tolerance for separateness, and space, as well as for an erotic privacy.

The bottom line is there are chances and risks either way for couples. Monogamy is not a static concept. Couples who are together thirty, forty years will in some sense have more than one marriage with each other. To survive, marriages have to be flexible, and sometimes flexibility will manifest around a renegotiation of sexual boundaries. Couples who do this purposefully seem to have sexually fulfilling relationships.

There are couples who are totally monogamous and haven't had sex in twenty-six years, and couples where in fifteen years only one spouse has initiated lovemaking. Some couples are willing to face the unknown; for others, change is massively anxiety-producing.

I dislike the terms "open" or "closed" marriages. That is fit for a door, not a relationship. People are not merely monogamous or non-monogamous. They can be mostly monogamous; periodically non-monogamous . . . there is a range. If we say "open" or "closed" we can say the open one wants to experience sexuality as expansive—with tenderness and connection.

Frank Pittman, MD:

You cannot be partway in the marriage. You must be in all the way. People can get depressed and not get joy from any aspect of their lives—job, children, car, as well as their relationships with spouses and friends and parents. By focusing their dissatisfaction solely on the marriage I assume the marriage is where they're not following through with their part of the commitment.

Sure, we feel attracted to other people. I've been married forty-eight years but have, for instance, been crazy in love with Meryl Streep, Juliet Binoche, and Susan Sarandon. It's fine to play with these attractions from a safe distance. Those who need to do something about it have no imagination, and fantasies can't suffice. This speaks to the notion that love has to be about craziness and excitement and danger rather than about receiving some sort of comfort from a partner.

In the lust stage the brain is full of sex hormones like testosterone. The effect is similar to a drug-induced high. There is not enough of the hormone oxytocin, associated with the ability to maintain healthy interpersonal relationships. The lack of oxytocin means this person is not capable of nurturing. You can feel great excitement but not enjoy compassion or generosity for anyone else. Look at it this way—Romeo shouldn't have crashed the party. It was bad for him and Juliet. While in the throes of lust you're willing to die together, which is pretty ridiculous. When you settle into a relationship, the influential hormones are oxytocin and vasopressin. These hormones make us territorial. We're at home.

Someone who operates on lust alone is not ready to become a grownup. Those hormones are a shield against entering into intimate domestic relationships on a meaningful level. A person who is unsatisfied in his or her marriage will also be unsatisfied by the next one . . . and the next. This is not a solution. This person is captivated by fantasy. This person doesn't want to insert his precious organs into someone who doesn't conform precisely to his fantasies. He is trying to use sex as an affirmation of sexuality rather than celebrating the relationship.

" MY TAKE "

This question goes to the heart of one of the biggest controversies surrounding theories about what a couple must be in order to have a shot at happiness and normalcy—eternally faithful. Both experts cited here are highly respected in the field. Dr. Pittman, whose book *Private Lies* is a classic in infidelity literature, and whose marriage has lasted forty-eight years, considers non-monogamy a cop-out, a nonstop craving for a Peter (or Petra) Pan amphetamine-like high. Romeo and Juliet should not be viewed as martyrs to a once-in-a-lifetime love, but as fools. Where Dr. Pittman loses a little momentum is in the rigidity and judgment expressed against someone "not ready to become a grownup." Must everyone subscribe to the same worldview? Must we all conduct ourselves in sync, with any misstep calling for a harsh jury pool?

Perel offers the "multicultural" viewpoint, which is more accepting of nuance, doubt, and flexibility—traits that seem admirable in politicians as well as marital partners. To her, marriage should perhaps entail a series of treaties couples draft as the years pass and their needs change. I admire her clinical style, assisting a couple in defining their definitions and boundaries rather than insinuating her own. And what longtime married couple has not experienced or inflicted a big or little betrayal that was trivialized as unimportant because it did not involve body parts? To Perel the best solution to the monogamy question is that the couple work together to come to an agreement with which they can coexist.

To further riff on the opinions presented here, search internally before opting for a quick fix, the easy hormonal high. Reflect on whether those yearnings to experience the taste of another are more about internal dissatisfaction than issues with the partner. Or, think about possible consequences, the risk to a basically happy marriage, as a result of indulging in the fleeting pleasures of a fling.

The question here should perhaps be changed to, "Can a marriage work if one partner wants monogamy and the other wants non-monogamy?" There are no easy answers, but both experts would agree that the betrayal of trust is the real villain here, not, as Dr. Pittman sassily put it, the "insertion of precious organs" where they don't belong.

A marriage may or may not ultimately succeed if it is sexually open, but it will definitely fail if the couple cannot be open about their hopes, dreams, and desires.

Why is my husband so turned on by pornography, and when should I regard it as a threat to our relationship?

DEBRA MANDEL, PhD:

Porn has become a major source of sexual difficulties for couples. It's usually a symptom of a bigger problem. For a man, pornography provides an easy "relationship" with no responsibility or strings attached. It's not quid pro pro—"I'll withhold sex unless you do A, B, and C." Men who are emotionally immature and/or in a marriage where sex is used "for trade" as reward or punishment can be lured by the nonemotional nature of looking at pictures on a porn site.

While he considers this behavior innocent—eroticism without complication—his wife might view her husband's desire for porn as a blow to her ego: "I'm not hot enough. He doesn't like my body."

Cybersex adds another layer as it has an emotional component. The husband might rationalize, "This isn't like hiring a prostitute. No one's underpants are involved, so it's not really cheating." But a man who e-mails or IMs a woman saying, "Oh, send a picture," or "I really love how you sound," is doing more than engaging in anonymous porn. He's searching for a connection that may be lacking in his marriage. Like women, men need validation, to be acknowledged and not to be criticized. But porn provides very intense stimulation, like a cocaine high. The man can become desensitized to his partner. He's being satiated elsewhere.

Porn is an addiction if it interferes with his life—i.e., he's spending his work day checking out porn sites or digging into his savings to pursue this "hobby." However, it needn't rise to the level of addiction for the marriage to be adversely affected. Both partners need to agree there is a problem and to care enough about the relationship to address it. It is human nature to want our partner's sexual energy reserved for us.

The couple must deal with the underlying resentment percolating between them. The wife should try not to personalize his attraction to porn, as very often it's more about his feeling shut out by her. The spouses must learn how to express themselves in a safe way (for example, to create relationship guidelines such as no name calling; putting a time limit on a discussion of a sensitive issue) and to consider trying new things in bed. Women have to get over the total romantic concept of lovemaking. Sometimes a guy just wants hardcore, fun, kinky sex.

Scott Haltzman, MD:

The answer to why men are turned on by porn should be obvious!

Many experts say this has nothing to do with men being attracted to women—there's an underlying psychological reason at play—but that's nonsense. On average, men have a higher sex drive for a variety of reasons. First, they have ten to twenty times more testosterone. Additionally, society puts pressure on boys being teased about whether they're getting sex, and media images project the idea that you're a man of significance if you get the beautiful woman. Finally, scientists believe men have more highly attuned visual centers in their brain, so images of attractive women can be very stimulating. Otherwise gentlemen's clubs and X-rated movies in hotel rooms wouldn't be so prevalent!

But there are different degrees of sexual stimulation garnered from looking at *Maxim* and Victoria's Secret catalogues to hardcore graphic images of S & M and other kinky sexual behavior. The issue isn't why a man is turned on by this, but whether he is using porn to an extent where it is interfering with his emotional and sexual connection with his wife. Some rough guidelines: Is he buying porn off the Internet or spending more than two hours a week looking at photos? The most important factor is whether he's less interested in sex with you. For example, is he stimulating himself with porn images soon after turning you down? The most important determinant—is he engaging in cybersex? Any exchange with a live person is proof he's gone too far.

In terms of setting up rules—you should let him enjoy the swimsuit issue of *Sports Illustrated*, but his e-mailing or IM-ing other women is a no-no. If clear-cut sexual addiction is an issue, there should be an absolute moratorium on porn material—even *SI*—and an insistence that he seek professional help.

So while it's not a fair assumption that his interest in porn has anything to do with your sexual relationship, it is a good idea to open up a dialogue about your sex life. This can be an opportunity to better define needs and expectations in an area couples seldom talk about.

For women, the equivalent of porn is romance novels. A wife reads about these incredible men, then looks at her husband and see an ordinary guy sitting around scratching his balls. Men in these books fulfill every woman's fantasy. That's not realistic either!

" MY TAKE "

There is a point/counterpoint-ish tinge to these comments:

- **Dr. Mandel:** A husband's predilection for porn is more about emotional erosion in the marriage than about sex drive.
- **Dr. Haltzman:** Blame or credit the testosterone factor.

Both make valid points. As a woman, I especially appreciated Dr. Haltzman's insistence that hey, nothing personal, men enjoy porn because, well, men enjoy porn! Each expert hammers home a similar message: Liking porn isn't necessarily the end of Western civilization or even the institution of marriage. The husband's fondness for erotica becomes problematic if it hampers, or turns into a substitute for, a connection with his wife. He's definitely crossing the line if he's venturing into cybersex territory. Obviously, if he is obsessed or addicted, do not pass GO; seek help.

Porn can be a catalyst that exacerbates small resentments and hurts that have been silently simmering, creating fertile conditions for this rift. A willingness to explore how this hobby might be adversely affecting the marriage creates an opportunity to open up the relationship. No, not that way, but by softening enough to communicate more honestly and empathetically, perhaps even broadening the range of marital lovemaking. And wives should ask themselves this question: Are there three people in your bed—you, hubby, and Fabio?

The prevalence, or rather virulence of Internet porn is reaching epic proportions. A study conducted by the American Academy of Matrimonial Lawyers found that a growing complaint among spouses filing for divorce is—you guessed it—cyberporn. It's not surprising then to learn that 8 percent to 10 percent of Internet users become hooked on cybersex. A corollary: Online infidelity often leads to offline sexual hookups.

I cite those statistics to give a not-so-subtle nudge about the importance of not taking your partner for granted, not putting him/her down, and taking the risk of being vulnerable. And hey, throw in the occasional sex toy.

How important is sex in a marriage anyway?

Ron Muchnick, PhD, and Sherri Muchnick, PhD:

Obviously there are many factors that are important in a marriage, sex being one of them. But it's not always about the physical act bringing a couple close. The important point is what sexuality represents—being connected, feeling intimate. That bond is what distinguishes a partner relationship from a friendship. Sexual expression usually helps foster that connection. Sometimes, though, it's other things that accomplish that trick. A patient, a woman in her fifties, said, "My husband cleaned the house without my asking. It was the best turn-on I've ever had."

It's important for each individual in the relationship to find his or her own sexuality level. There is no right or wrong way to do anything. We've worked with couples who haven't had sex in five to ten years and are happy. These couples have fun together, a shared vision, shared goals, perhaps they're raising children together, and those are the things that make them feel intimate.

In most healthy relationships, though, sex is a factor. Couples should strive to keep lovemaking fresh and satisfactory for both.

Stephen W. Simpson, PhD:

On the one hand our culture gives us the message that sex is the most important thing. Couples will respond to this by saying it's not really that big a deal. But sex is important in ways that aren't often realized. Having a healthy sex life is foundational. Even when a couple I'm treating doesn't bring up sex as a problem, I ask how often they have sex. The answer can be surprising: "Well, it's been a year and a half." That tells me there's a hidden level of dysfunction.

We experience the world through our bodies. If a healthy physical intimacy is lacking, there's a whole piece of the relationship that's missing. That lack affects everything! I'm not saying you have to have sex three times a day or even three times a week. A healthy sex life means different frequencies for different couples.

If a couple have a good emotional attachment it doesn't matter if their sex drives aren't evenly matched. Let's say a husband wishes there was more sex. But he feels loved by his wife, so if she's not in the mood he's not injured. When the mismatch becomes a point of conflict, there are always other issues.

In those instances when one partner wants more sex it's symbolic of another area where intimacy seems to be lacking. Perhaps he or she feels the spouse isn't really committed to the relationship. It's rare that these differences in drive are purely about hormones. There's some insecurity, a lack of self-esteem.

The notion of a celibate marriage is silly. Sex is essential to a healthy relationship.

" MY TAKE "

While both experts believe that good sex is a vital component in most healthy relationships, they subsequently diverge. Dr. Ron Muchnick and Dr. Sherri Muchnick feel that the true connective tissue is shared intimacy, and that the expression of same needn't be physical. Their female patient apparently finds that her husband doing a chore she hates is more of a turn-on than is an appropriately placed vibrator. Dr. Simpson says if a couple feels they can be happy sans sex, they're delusional.

The truth to my mind lies somewhere in the middle, tilting closer to Dr. Simpson's point of view. During a long-term relationship there will inevitably be periods when other things have priority over sex—jobs, children, time pressure. But the need to physically express love for one another is ever-present, even if under the surface.

Again I tilt toward Dr. Simpson's perspective that when differences in sex drive arise it's usually a symptom of a "disease" in the relationship. But sometimes one person is simply more highly sexed than the other. In those cases negotiations should be conducted. For instance, the person who is not in the mood can occasionally agree to have sex anyway. And/or the more uninterested person might suggest experimenting with some new techniques. Oftentimes sexual boredom is at the core of a sexual stalemate.

Say both partners agree the lack of sex isn't a problem. Still, every once in a while one or both wonder, "How long has it been since we've had some form of physical intimacy?" If it's necessary to count not just fingers and toes but the fingers and toes of the partner as well as of various neighbors—Houston, there is a problem.

Life is full of commitments and stresses, but a committed couple must make quality time together a priority. That means making time on a regular basis to discuss needs, expectations, and dreams. Otherwise anger and resentment will build. It's also crucial to do enjoyable activities together that can build memories. This includes sexy activities. Watch porn, text dirty messages, go to an X-rated hotel. Sure, fires bank after the initial honeymoon phase, but couples should never allow sex to linger too long on the back burner.

What are some sexual techniques we can incorporate into our admittedly limited repertoire?

DIANA KIRSCHNER, PHD:

Discover each other all over again. Have ten-minute listening sessions where one person gets to talk, free-associate, and say whatever is on his or her mind. The listener does not speak. No matter what, use a clock and honor a full ten-minute session. Then switch roles. Anything said in that time is sacred and cannot be brought up during an argument! You never will know your partner's world until you really listen. And intimacy opens the gate to passion.

Play Sexy Dress-Up. Let your fantasies go wild by finding sexy lingerie and other sexy play outfits. Dress up and role-play being the nurse, doctor, maid, dominatrix, vixen, or sex slave, and create a hot escapade that is entirely different from your normal sexual routine.

Be Dessert for Each Other. Get naked, grab the whipped cream or chocolate syrup, and make yourself into a sumptuous dessert for your partner. Make sure you lather it on in the areas of your body that give you the most pleasure.

Play Strip Poker. The loser of the hand takes off an article of clothing, reveals a secret, or describes a sexual fantasy. If you win, you can ask your partner to take off all of his/her clothes at once. But if you lose . . . well, you get the idea. Either way, there are no losers.

Isadora Alman:

This couple needs to look at their usual routine—who initiates, who does what to whom, and for roughly how long? Are they strictly missionary in the dark? In that case, the whole world can open if they turn on the light. They need some education. It would be helpful to rent Sinclair Institute's *Better Sex Videos* (*www.sinclairinstitute.com*), which are excellent and also customized—there are some geared to young couples, black couples, fat couples, etc.!

The videos can be viewed alone or together. There are also many good books, everything from *The Joy of Sex* to the *Kama Sutra* and Gregory Stock's *Book of Questions: Love & Sex*.

Each person should make a private wish list—"I think I'd like to try X and would definitely like to try Z." Rather than exchange lists, be creative. For example, "I just won a hand of bridge. The prize I want is light bondage." Or, "Let's make a bet how many blue cars we pass on the way to the freeway. The one who comes closest gets to control the evening's entertainment." Establish a playfulness while bettering your ability to communicate. Other suggestions for couples in a rut—go to a nude beach, a swing club (to watch, not participate), and/or take a marriage enrichment course through the Human Awareness Institute (*www.hai.org*), which offers weekend workshops at various locations around the country.

" MY TAKE "

Once the initial pow of passion fades it is important to inject creativity into the mix lest sex becomes mired in a rut: Hit the same two or three erogenous zones, climax, and call it a night. Happily, the advice of both experts is on-point and relatively easy to implement. However, Alman gives some creative and specific resources. Help is out there. And why wait for your relationship to be in trouble before taking a couples' workshop?

Think back to those single days when it seemed a gigantic stroke of luck to net a casual alliance with someone bearing a strong resemblance to whichever half of Brangelina holds most appeal. Sure, the first few times were wildly exciting. But if there was no "underneath" to the relationship, no connective tissue other than the outer layer, didn't the sizzle—sooner rather than later—fizzle?

Committed, long-term passion has the potential to remain fiery year after year, decade after decade, if partners trust one another enough to be completely vulnerable and honest. Studies show the most sexually satisfied of all are married couples in the early AARP demographic—fifty to fifty-nine. Makes sense. If two people are with the one person who knows them inside and out there is no fear of judgment, of casting aside inhibitions, of being rejected—there is no fear. In mutual fearlessness lie the fruits of mutual victory.

Another "secret" ingredient no doubt shared by couples in the study: the realization that sex is not do-or-die. Sometimes love-making is mind- and soul-blowing; other times a person can obsess over the cranky toddler wailing through the thin wall, or occasion-ally wish his or her beloved would finish before the *Tonight Show*; and once in a while that erection is MIA. No matter—overall, being together is fun. A new position was a disaster? What a giggle! Spread the news: The ultimate aphrodisiac is shared laughter.

Finally, stay connected day to day. Being unplugged from one another emotionally inevitably takes its toll in the bedroom. "It might feel genital," writes Dr. Daniel Amen in *Sex on the Brain*, "but the vast majority of sex and love occur in the brain."

Why am I not sexually attractive to my husband (or how can I be more sexually attractive)?

Stephanie Buehler, MSW, PsyD, CST:

Sometimes people marry someone to whom they're not sexually attracted. This typically happens because the "non-sexy" person offers emotional and/or financial safety and security. The person is viewed as having many wonderful qualities, although chemistry is not one of them. This isn't something that can be fixed—that "Oh my God, I've got to have you" feeling is either there or not there.

I advise people in these kinds of relationships to think of it as akin to an arranged marriage. The problem is common with both men and women. For instance, a man will marry a woman he sees as stable—she's a pleasant person, he's just emerged from a toxic divorce, he's not hugely attracted to her but he's not grossed out. It's like your parents picked someone out for you. Hopefully you'll become more physically attracted over time as you fall in love with who he or she is inside. But you can't create magic if it was never there in the first place.

If it's a case of your partner not being as attracted to you as he or she once was, well, people do change in their physical appearance as well as who they are emotionally. Your partner could have a lot of unexpressed resentment, which is taking its toll in the bedroom. Good communication needs to be established with the resentful partner learning to express emotions and the other person learning how to listen or at least be less rigid. Couples therapy can help.

Sexual desire or lack of it can be about power. The one who doesn't want sex or wants it infrequently has the control. Often it's the only area in the relationship where this person feels he or she has some control. Sometimes a woman loses interest because her husband is clumsy in the bedroom or not a mind reader. She can become enraged over this and feel contempt. Here is another area where therapy can help.

Or perhaps the culprit is your partner being under a lot of stress, perhaps feeling spread too thin. In these instances it's helpful to brainstorm ways to change one's lifestyle. Say you're a working mom. Consider arranging with your husband the opportunity two times a week after dinner to put your feet up and take a break. He can handle child care for an hour or two. If he feels this will result in sex, he'll be cooperative. Other suggestions: Get someone to clean the house and start saying no to time-consuming extra projects.

MICHELE WEINER-DAVIS, MSW:

There's a big difference between whether this lack of attraction is something new or something that's always existed. Generally the attraction is hottest in the beginning. What's changed? Perhaps the couple now has children, so it's harder to be spontaneous. Some planned spontaneity can be helpful. They should arrange a time when they can be without the kids. There are also situations where the husband is attracted to his wife and then she becomes a mother and totally immersed in child care and he starts viewing her less as a lover.

Sometimes I'll hear, "Well, my spouse was attracted to me when I was thirty pounds thinner." This sounds shallow and non-PC, but the truth is attraction is a very primal thing. Perhaps the relationship isn't as important to this person anymore, so she's not making an effort to be visually appealing to her mate.

The wife can look beyond herself to possible reasons for his lack of interest. Perhaps there are biological factors—a cardiovascular problem, an illness, he might be on antidepressants that affect hormonal fluctuation. Being depressed can certainly dampen his desire. Did he have a traumatic childhood that he has been suppressing? In the beginning things seemed fine in the marriage, but then unresolved issues from the past kicked back up.

Additionally, interpersonal issues between the couple can contribute to this problem. It's not just women who don't want to have sex if they're not close emotionally to their partner. A wife who is frequently highly critical, resentful, and/or angry at her husband is a real desire buster for a man.

These things can be fixable. It's tricky because in our culture we tend to equate virility and masculinity. Men are mortified to talk about this problem, even to their wife. So many women feel they're the only ones in the world whose husbands aren't chasing them around the dining room table. They take personal responsibility and feel unattractive, unloved, and unwanted.

If he won't at least get a physical, be proactive. Make the appointment and make sure he gets in the car. Don't worry.

You're not turning into his mother. You're helping him and your marriage.

" MY TAKE "

Weiner-Davis touches lightly on the dreaded, "My partner never had the hots for me" scenario. Dr. Buehler offers a bit more, likening the situation to an arranged marriage and offering advice that focuses on how a loved but not lusted-after partner's inner beauty might eventually radiate outward.

The experts are more sanguine and prescriptive on what they view as the more "fixable" problem. Dr. Buehler states that the trifecta of poor communication, grab for power, and/or stress of daily life can contribute to the withering of a once-powerful sexual bond. Weiner-Davis points out other potential factors that dampen libido. For instance, a spouse who's packed on the pounds can find that his or her partner's passion is not unconditional. But the weight gain can be a subtle signal that it's no longer important to look good. It's also important to look beyond feelings of rejection to consider that the mate's lack of sexual desire might be a side effect of physical and/or emotional problems that are not about the partnership.

Dr. Buehler and Weiner-Davis both advocate seeking solutions for the problem, ranging from developing better communication skills to devoting less attention to dust balls.

Let me throw some paint at the canvas and see what resonates. If a spouse has never been sexually attracted to his mate in more than a perfunctory way, here's a tough question: Is he into women? There are men who are gay or bi but enter heterosexual marriages. That's okay as long as both people are cognizant of all the facts.

There are also instances where a person is not highly sexed, so physical attraction to his or her mate isn't high on the priority list. However, while this may be a workable "contract" for one-half of the couple, it may be untenable for the other. This is why needs, expectations, and hopes for a mutually happy sex life should be shared sooner versus later. Even worse than feeling that one's partner is sexually indifferent is to attack oneself for not having what it takes to turn someone on.

Or is the husband definitely hot for women but cool toward his partner? If this is the case, ask what qualities he considers sexy. I'm not suggesting subverting one's essence, but rather beginning the process of opening up, discovering different facets—facets he will appreciate. Share idiosyncratic sexual preferences with him as well. And why not add some experimentation into the mix? This is advice that is also ideal for a couple when one partner has slowly lost interest. Try new techniques, new settings. The right spices add flavor and pizzazz to a lot more than food.

We've been married seven years and our sex life is fine, sometimes great, but how I wish it could at least on occasion be a transformative experience, where it wasn't just bodies pleasuring each other, but we felt as one. Is this possible, or only a Hollywood fantasy?

Pat Love, EdD:

To transform sex in a long-term relationship you need to add novelty and/or a little danger, fear, or risk. You must always risk in the direction of your partner, meaning the risk must be something you know he or she will like but which is a little scary or risky for you to give or initiate. For instance, you can take the risk of initiating sex in a different location or at a different time than usual. Or, perhaps for the first time ever, wear no underwear or send a romantic e-mail or text. Or the risk can be in the form of intimacy as in completing the following sentences:

- If you weren't in my life I would miss. . . .
- I love it when you. . . .
- It's a turn-on for me when you. . . .
- It might be fun for us to try. . . .

Basically I'm suggesting you do something out of character. The novelty wakes up the brain and releases dopamine, which heightens your senses. It works this way: The brain is programmed to pay attention to anything new or different until it figures out you're "safe," at which point that adrenaline rush stops. That's why it's important to keep taking these small romantic risks in an ongoing relationship. Then things remain exciting and never too "safe."

JUDY KURIANSKY, PHD:

I recommend tantric sex. It's a practice that started in the East more than 5,000 years ago. It increases intimacy and brings the "energy" exchange during sex to a high level.

The basic activity is to create a night that's very special. Beautify your environment: Add a different-colored light bulb, a different bedspread; light candles. Bathe each other. Be exceptionally clean. Then both of you should put on special clothes that make you feel like a god and goddess. This helps you find the divinity within one another.

When you come together in the lovemaking space, make a dedication: "We intend to be really present with each other for this lovemaking and to feel higher states of ecstasy and enlightenment."

The breath is the key to extending the length of pleasure and being able to direct that pleasure so that you have orgasms in different places—knees, elbows, eyes, toes—and the orgasms are deeper.

To synchronize your energies, look deeply into one another's eyes and breathe in and out simultaneously. Do the synchronized breaths for however long feels right—four minutes, ten minutes. As you are breathing, imagine sending love energy to your partner. Then put your hands on different parts of your partner's body and send love energy to those places. Stimulate each other as in regular sex but hesitate in the middle and breathe and send energy into those places you are stimulating.

In addition to extending lovemaking, this practice is quite magical. It brings you to a "higher" place together. Whatever space you think a bottle of wine gets you to—this brings you to a much better, truly connected place. And you can start this practice whether you're newlyweds or married twenty years.

" MY TAKE "

Transforming sex is possible when you go outside of your comfort zone, according to both experts. The appropriately named Dr. Love advocates risk-taking as a way to trigger dopamine, a.k.a. a hormone-induced high. I heartily agree that it's important to allow yourself to be vulnerable. The beauty of a long-term relationship is that ideally, you trust your partner enough to feel that it's safe to take a risk. Don't settle for same old, same old and then resent your partner for being boring in bed.

Dr. Kuriansky's primer on the possibilities of tantric sex (check out her book, listed in Appendix B, for a more thorough explanation) can intrigue couples enough to try this sacred form of lovemaking. Tantric sex—which is about gaining control over your energy—assists men in delaying ejaculation, leading to deep and multiple orgasms, and helps couples regard the whole sexual experience as joyful and not just a build-up to climaxing. Tantra says that if you focus on the journey with one another the trip can be a blast, transcendentally speaking. If you feel that tantric sex seems like too much work and trouble, just take five minutes and gaze silently into each other's eyes. You will be staring not just at a face you know as well as your own, but supposedly at a window into your own soul.

The point here is not what technique a couple tries, but that they take on this "mission" of sexual rejuvenation as a joint project. Without adversely critiquing your partner's sexual acumen, suggest trying a few specific techniques in bed. Ask for some suggestions as well.

Undertake this journey with real intent, not half-resigned that things will never change; that you know every move in each other's repertoire; that neither body involved is that of a sex god. Change is possible if a couple truly believes it to be. Make only a half-hearted effort—maybe light a scented candle but not expect anything to feel different—and it will become the same old moves except for the presence of a sweet-smelling candle.

FIELD REPORT

With two children and two jobs, we were always exhausted and behind the eight ball. There was never enough time to accomplish everything that needed doing. Making love took a backseat. This was something that upset both of us since we'd always had great chemistry together. The solution—making "sex dates." Sometime it's two hours, occasionally a whole evening or—joy of joys if we get a babysitter—an overnight trip. Planning passion revitalized our marriage. Who says only spontaneity is sexy?

~Keela Thomas, 33, Las Vegas, Nevada

IF I HAD A DO-OVER

Keith Newcombe
Nashville, Tennessee

"You can't make someone love you"

I married in 1993 after a two-year engagement. I was twenty-six, my wife thirty-one. What was the marriage like? I'd be home and my wife would walk in the door and greet the dog and not me.

We rarely had sex and when we did it was excruciatingly awful, like embracing a corpse. It was so bad I wept.

I wasn't trying to be a martyr, but I'd made a vow and intended to be married for life.

At some point my wife suggested marriage counseling. I went into it hoping to revive the relationship. The counselor pointed out my spouse probably wanted permission to end the marriage.

My hopes during the seven months of counseling were things like "I hope we can have dinner together every night." My wife would say, "Can you believe he actually wants to have dinner together every night?"

We took a trip together. I thought that helped us turn a corner but right afterward, during a session, she asked for a divorce.

Receiving the papers a month later was a turning point. I'd done everything humanly possible to make things work, but the person I'd viewed as my partner in life now regarded me as an enemy.

I went into individual therapy and came to see that I'd never been proactive in choosing partners. I'd never thought about the type of person I wanted. I'd let women pick me.

The divorce was final in 2000. I made a vow never again to get involved with someone that was ambivalent about her feelings. I needed to be with a woman who felt as deeply about me as I did about her. I found that woman. We've been married five wonderful years.

If your spouse doesn't want to be with you, it's okay to end the marriage because it doesn't really exist except on paper. Partners need to be married to one another in heart, body, and soul.

CHAPTER FOUR

BE PARTNERS AND PARENTS

I t can be problematic enough for couples to maintain a nurturing relationship when they only need to nurture one another. Adding children to the mix increases not only the joys, but also the pressures. Many partners become overwhelmed by the responsibilities of parenthood and lose the spark that once blazed between them. The experts address this dilemma as well as other serious problems that arise when two become three, including parents who undermine one another in front of the children and—tough love is necessary to prevent this one!—allowing offspring to witness fights.

Our parenting styles don't mesh. In my opinion my husband is way too permissive, leaving me to come across as the "mean" one. Even worse, he undermines me in their presence. He doesn't think there's a problem. What can I do?

CLOÉ MADANES, PHD, FAPA:

It's good for parents to have different viewpoints. Children need to understand that the world is complicated. In their lives they will have teachers with different ideas, employers with different ideas, and so on, and they will have to learn how to negotiate this.

Typically the dynamic is one parent being lenient while the other is strict. This doesn't mean the strict one is the bad guy. He or she could be seen as more the protector. This woman shouldn't experience her husband's position as undermining her. He is expressing his love in a different way. The parents don't have to be in total agreement all the time. What's important is for them to decide on five or six major issues. No violence, no stealing, anything that concerns safety. For example, it might provoke anxiety in the mother to hear her spouse say to their children, "Oh, it doesn't matter what time you come home."

The couple should have weekly "executive meetings" on an ongoing basis to discuss serious issues. At the meeting they might negotiate parenting strategies. The wife might say, "I cannot give in to the kids coming home after dark. It makes me too nervous." In exchange for her husband conceding this point, she might give permission for the children to dress more casually than she'd prefer. During these meetings it should be noted that one parent cannot dispute what the other says in front of the children. This keeps the kids from playing one parent against the other. Mommy and daddy have different opinions, but mommy and daddy are also a team.

So a certain level of disagreement is fine for the kids to witness. The children know daddy is more easygoing but also that the father will say, "I'm not going to give you permission unless your mother does."

SHARON M. RIVKIN, MA, MFT:

Couples have different parenting styles because they've been parented differently. What's important is not to be polarizing. If the husband is very permissive, the wife in turn becomes "the mean one" who just keeps insisting the husband become stricter. This dynamic gets them nowhere. And what is essential is that neither parent undermine the other in front of the children.

The wife needs to understand why her husband is permissive. This involves getting to the underlying issue. She should engage rather than attack him. For instance, she can say, "I see it's important to you to be a permissive father. What's that's about?" He might answer, "My parents were always mean and I don't want to do that to my kids." She starts to see he's a human being; he's got feelings! In turn, perhaps she came from a permissive family and thus has a need to set boundaries.

The real issue isn't that he's permissive and she's mean. The same dynamic is probably present in all their arguments. She feels not heard and he feels not appreciated. He works so hard doing so many things for the family. He just wants to have fun with the kids. Or he wants to be the good guy and keep things easy, so is passive aggressive and doesn't want to acknowledge there's a problem. She takes the bait and makes the decision, feeling like the mean one. Then he gets mad at the decision she made.

It's hard to change a lifetime pattern. Instead we just get louder, proclaiming our rigid views. I tell couples to change one small thing. Baby steps count. So the next time he undermines her in front of the children, rather than continuing the argument the wife can say when they're alone together, "Hey, I'm curious where you're coming from."

" MY TAKE "

Apparently, parenting is not kid stuff. And kids shouldn't be treated . . . well, like kids, according to Dr. Madanes, who insists that the small ones not be coddled or left to believe in a utopian world where people agree 100 percent of the time. What's next? Revealing that Santa Claus is a myth? Seriously, I love the therapist's contention that children need to learn that life sometimes (okay, frequently) involves coping with dissension. The proviso is this: At no time should the children be made to feel insecure or unsafe, fearful that agreeing with one parent will upset the other. I also endorse Dr. Madanes's suggestion that the parents vet the discipline issues most crucial to each, and then agree to compromise on the others.

Rivkin makes wonderful sense when she points out that the rift between mother and father extends well beyond their child-rearing beliefs. The dynamic between the couple extends throughout their relationship. People are ruled by patterns from their childhoods, and exploring what has shaped them rather than ceaselessly trying to change or ignore each other will better serve the whole family.

Don't put children in the position of being your confidante "tattling" on your partner: "Oh, I wish daddy would understand that I'm not overprotective with you but that it's dangerous out there." Or: "I hope the man you marry will be more romantic than daddy." Kids are not referees. They need your guidance, not to be your guidance counselors.

Our sex life used to be uninhibited and amazing. Ever since we became parents—we have a seven-year-old and a four-year-old—it's become boring and predictable. My wife screams at me if I get too loud. She's afraid the kids will hear. I want to keep my family together, but I'm beginning to think the only way to do that is to have an affair. Am I wrong?

MARION SOLOMON, PhD:

Having children changes the relationship between the mother and her husband. A lot of men have difficulty with this, as they want the mother to be available to them. According to attachment theory, women fall totally in love with their babies to the exclusion of everything else. In a good relationship both partners recognize this is a normal phase. But if the husband feels he's lost the person with whom he fell in love, he feels left out. It's an emotional as much as a sexual problem. For her part, the wife might feel the husband is demanding, which makes her lose interest in sex. She doesn't feel romanticized. She's angry. By the time the children are ages four, five, six, the pattern might be set. The wife says, "You're not treating me right. Why do you expect sex?" He withdraws.

Neither is looking at the way the other one feels. They're not looking at what happens during the interactions between them that is causing this distance. The problem isn't him or her but what they ended up doing when the kids were born, being so focused on their own needs. A wonderful book that can help couples in this trap is *Hold Me Tight: Seven Conversations for a Lifetime of Love* by Sue Johnson.

It's about looking at the problem in different ways. It's not that he's demanding sexually and she's a cold bitch. Each person behaves in a certain way when their needs are not met. If you feel that someone doesn't care about your welfare, at some point you will turn off. Sex will dry up. There will be hurt and danger and blaming.

Having an affair is almost a sure way to distance your partner. It won't help the relationship. What will help is to manipulate the relationship with the purpose of re-creating romance. For instance, when my husband and I had little children, on occasion we'd go to a hotel from 8 P.M. to 10 P.M. The point is, you need some alone time together. Couples really have to put a lot of energy into making the relationship work.

ESTHER PEREL:

The idea that sex makes babies, and babies are an erotic disaster for couples, is ironic. Family life thrives on routine, consistency, regularity, and predictability. Eroticism is fueled by mystery, the unexpected, and novelty. In a way, what eroticism thrives on is what family life defends against. That's one reason it is so difficult to bring lust home.

In addition, many people grew up in homes where they did not experience healthy sexuality. So after having children, couples don't know how to let romance work its way back into the fabric of life. But sex is fun. It feels good. It makes us closer. Reclaiming eroticism isn't always easy. Part of it has to do with the importance or lack thereof people attribute to it. Many couples will virtually schedule sex out of their relationships; it's on permanent standby while they attend to more pressing matters.

But today, families only survive if the couple is happy. There is no other mandate keeping couples together but mutual fulfillment, especially once the children are grown. This puts parents in a bind. They want perfect children and so attend to the children's every need. There is a clash between child centrality that is unfolding against the backdrop of romanticism. Couples talk to me about how they have become like a management company. For instance, they feel guilty about closing their bedroom door, and many seem to have trouble finding a babysitter, even when their own parents had no trouble doing so.

Couples who experience erotic intimacy after having children are willful and intentional about it. It's not that it comes easy, but they understand the importance of keeping erotic energy alive and well. When you look at erotic ingredients like playfulness, creativity, fun—all those have been redirected at the kids. Some of it needs to be brought back to the relationship. It is not the children who extinguish the flame; it is parents who fail to keep the spark alive.

Cultivating the erotic bond between partners requires care and attention that competes with the over-centrality of children that characterizes the dominant parenting ideology of the day.

For many parents, the idea of being sexual in their home goes against a certain puritanical tradition. It brings up acute guilt and anxiety, as though our adult sexuality would be inappropriate or dangerous for the children. But who are we protecting? When children see their primary caregivers expressing affection discreetly and appropriately, they're more likely to grow up with a sense of healthy sexuality.

The wife of this letter writer is afraid her kids will wake up if she and her husband have noisy sex. But if we censor ourselves, what we end up transmitting to our children is our inhibitions. With a generation that favors hookups or friends with benefits, you need a place to look at sex in the context of a loving relationship, and to understand that mother and father are not just parents, but sexual partners.

" MY TAKE "

Both experts agree that parenthood is a game changer for couples on the intimacy front—alas, only occasionally for the better.

Dr. Solomon warns that distancing patterns can set in soon after the birth. The husband feels left out, a third wheel, while the wife's primary emotion concerning her spouse is irritation at his lack of understanding for what she's experiencing. This dissonance is an underground burr, with both parties becoming more and more estranged. As Dr. Solomon rightly suggests, it's essential for couples to summon the energy to bring fresh eyes to the deadlocked situation (not a fresh body; cheating not advised!). However, with—as the therapist puts it—"hurt and danger and blaming" the norm, finding said energy can feel as impossible as pushing a boulder uphill. Putting aside an evening to reminisce about the past and recall amorous nights and romantic holidays can be a springboard to creating a blueprint to carve out "alone time" on an ongoing basis.

Perel points out that family life and mind-bending sex are incompatible. You can't "attack" each other with abandon in every room of the house when little pitchers have big ears. Additionally, the couples and family therapist rails against an overarching "puritanical tradition" in America that has parents too guilt-ridden to role-model for their children what a healthy sexual partnership can look like. Parents should heed Perel's passionate argument that transmitting inhibitions rather than unashamed (but not blatant) shows of affection to one's children can have negative consequences—for example, resulting in the young'uns subsequently dissociating sex from committed relationships.

Both experts believe that, as Perel puts it, couples must be "willful and intentional" about remaining enthusiastic sex partners lest they devolve into being co-parents and nothing more.

Just as parents take pride in their children's accomplishments, for example by putting finger paintings and report cards on the fridge, they should make the time and energy to create and mark pivotal couple milestones. This means doing things together that don't involve the children—anything from engaging in volunteer work to taking out gym memberships to enrolling in dance classes. Then celebrate their triumphs—make a date to tango the night away, shop for new "thin" clothes after the gym works its magic, and so on.

And learn new sex tricks together—buy videos and toys, read erotica together (more Anaïs Nin than *Penthouse*), have a night of prolonged foreplay. These tricks of course do necessitate having a lock on the bedroom door!

My husband and I can't seem to stop arguing in front of the kids. Any advice on how to stop?

BEVERLY SMALLWOOD, PHD:

Destructive arguing has no place within earshot of children. Not only are you modeling these patterns for them to adopt now and in their future relationships, but also you are creating an insecure environment for them. Their parents are their anchors. If kids are always wondering if the next news is divorce, this can have an impact on all areas of their lives. Children who live in chaotic homes fare worse in academic performance, personal relationships, and self-esteem.

If you and your spouse are having trouble controlling your tempers, your behavior suggests that when you "get going," you are so caught up in winning that you lose sight of what's really important. Not only does that bode poorly for your kids; it also is not a good sign that you have even a chance of resolving your issues successfully.

It's time for the two of you to learn better skills for "fighting," more constructively known as problem solving. In other words, one problem is what you're doing in front of the kids. Another problem is what you're doing and how you're doing it. Are you attacking the problem, or attacking each other? Do you drag up the past, or do you focus on what's happening now so that it can be changed today? Are you calmly describing your perceptions, making suggestions for change, and negotiating solutions? Are you really listening to each other, or jumping to conclusions and interrupting? Are you set on "scoring points," which is the foundation of a win-lose strategy, or are you set on helping each other win by creating an action plan that enables both of you to get at least some of what you need and want?

If you get really good at problem solving—which you need to do whether or not tender ears are listening—it wouldn't hurt the kids to sometimes see you discussing things calmly, negotiating and reaching a workable solution. That's a model they need! But right now, make a couple of pacts with your husband:

- We'll get professional coaching on fighting more fairly.
- Let's agree that when we feel tensions rising, our immediate desire to strike out at each other will be absolutely trumped by the needs of our children.
- We'll develop a time-out signal, and then set a time to talk when we can do so privately.

This last agreement will not only help with the immediate problem; it will allow both of you to calm down, think, organize your thoughts, and choose to discuss the situation reasonably.

STEVEN STOSNY, PHD:

Children remind you of what's important. Whatever you're disagreeing about is not as important as the welfare of the children. That's a core value. The only exception is if the kids see you first argue, then kiss and make up. This shows them your bond is resilient. But parents typically argue in front of the kids, send them to bed, and then make up. That's harmful parenting.

I train couples to hide their arguing, and keep their voices down in front of the children. I've never seen a relationship where kids are unaware of problems between their parents; they sense the tension. In fact, kids monitor the emotions of their parents more closely than their own, especially young children. The only thing little ones can do for their survival is attach to someone who will care for them. If parents don't care properly for the children, their survival is threatened.

So try to work out the problem. Again, what means more, the kids or the disagreement? Problem solving isn't the hard part. What's hard is having a compassionate understanding of your partner while the two of you are caught in a disagreement.

First, you have to hold on to your self-value when you don't like your partner's behavior. That behavior is not devaluing you. If he or she is ignoring you, it's not about you—meaning it doesn't make you less worthwhile, though of course you want to feel valued by the person you love.

The second-hardest thing is to hold on to the value you feel toward your partner when you don't like his or her behavior. Do you think you'll be more successful engaging your spouse when you're regarding him or her with value and respect or when you're feeling angry at being ignored?

" MY TAKE "

Good advice here geared toward helping a couple stop acting like children, at least in the presence of their children. Dr. Smallwood explains that the inability to rein in one's worst impulses and exhibit some discretion speaks to winning and feeling "right" as being a voracious, ungovernable need. She points to the urgency of learning to solve problems together rather than pairing up to cause problems sure to merit future psychiatric bills for the kids. I like her distinction that this doesn't mean never letting the kids witness parents disagreeing, provided things are subsequently worked out in reasonable fashion. But never dissolve into tantrum-throwing adversaries within earshot of small fry.

Dr. Stosny is also a proponent of the value of letting kids see parents civilly disagree. He brings up the vital capper that it's important to go full circle and allow the G-rated kiss-and-make-up part of the scenario to be witnessed as well. It's also important to separate your upset over the disagreement about a particular issue from your overall feelings about the marriage. You can agree to sometimes disagree without it shaking the foundation of the relationship.

Again, as long as a couple act responsibly, it's not a problem to occasionally argue in front of the children. If in an attempt to protect the kids from conflict the parents never disagree in front of them, the lesson imparted is to avoid dissension. They will also be forgoing other lessons, such as how to be tolerant, accept differences, and to forgive.

As Dr. Stosny points out, children can be more aware when something is amiss between their parents than are their parents! Since kids are so hypervigilant and overly sensitive, it's important to notice how they behave during and after witnessing a fight. Some children try to be referees, interceding between the parents. Or they become fearful or depressed or act rude or cold toward mommy and/or daddy. It's important to reassure them that they are not to blame and to show them that there are no lingering hurt feelings, that the love and respect between their parents remains as strong as ever.

Nine months after our child was born I feel like my wife has practically forgotten my existence. I know our priorities are different now, and of course I love my daughter. But it seems like my wife is uninterested in making time for me. How can I get her to stop treating me like a third wheel?

WILLIAM J. DOHERTY, PhD:

This is very complicated. If a man gets into a whiny mode—Why don't you have time for me?—his wife might start feeling like she has another child. It's not that he shouldn't pay attention to his feeling of being deprived and neglected, but the challenge is to bring this up in a constructive way and offer to problem-solve with her. What can he do to help out more with child care or housework?

What the wife should realize is that just because she's now a mother doesn't mean she's not still part of a marriage. Perhaps she feels that because her husband is an adult he doesn't need her as much as the child does. This kind of thinking can lead her to essentially "marry" the child. If her only reaction to her husband's point of view—"You're so tired. We never have sex. I don't mean as much to you anymore"—is "Grow up, buddy," more distance will be created in the marriage. A little empathy is helpful on her part.

The couple should try for little rituals—a nightly cup of tea together, cuddling before falling asleep even if she's too tired for sex, hiring the occasional sitter so they can go out on a date. Offer little appreciations for one another. Say, "I love you" frequently. Keep kissing and touching. Becoming parents needn't mean you're no longer a couple.

JONATHAN ALPERT:

For nine months the wife experienced intense changes, which helped prepare her for the enormity of what's to come. For her mate, the birth is when the realization hits that life as he knew it is over.

The sexual dynamic between the couple changes. She may not be feeling attractive and/or she's not in the mood. She's consumed and overwhelmed and insecure on many levels and doesn't have energy for the relationship. I'm not saying this is common, but I've seen cases of infidelity on the part of the husband at this time.

He should offer praise about her mothering abilities and comments about what he finds attractive about her in this phase of their lives together. Go slowly. Do little things like giving her a shoulder rub. Be aware that since the pregnancy began her body has been undergoing hormonal fluctuations that cause emotional as well as physical changes that impact the couple. There is a third person in the relationship now. The husband has to begin to accept the change and the accompanying responsibilities.

It's hard for her to be spontaneous. The baby is waking up in the middle of the night needing to be tended to. The husband should come up with a plan to help ease her stress. For instance, on Sundays he can offer to do the grocery shopping. This is a good time to be creative and discover healthy ways to have his needs met. He can find something to do independently during the time he and his wife used to curl up to watch TV . . . and think up activities to do as a family.

Often the husband is in denial, not wanting things to change. He is grieving the loss of his youth and independence. He should talk to male friends who have children to get an idea of what it's like to be a father. When tensions arise, have the awareness that it's not his wife's fault. There are many changes going on, and adjustments need to be made.

" MY TAKE "

It's clear the therapists answering this question are male, as their focus is on helping the husband realize he needs to "help out." A female might have pointed out that since the husband is 50 percent responsible for creating the baby, he might consider taking on the same percentage of responsibility when it comes to divvying up child care and household chores.

That said, there are good take-home lessons here. Dr. Doherty's assertion that being whiny will result in exasperating the wife to the point of feeling like she's dealing with a "Terrible Two" is a money shot. The husband needs to step up in ways both constructive and creative to make his partner feel she's not in this alone. I particularly like the idea of creating little ongoing rituals as a way of maintaining intimacy. And difficult as the task may be in her stressed-out, over-tired state, it would be helpful for the new mother to realize that her husband is not feeling bereft to annoy her or make her feel guilty, but because he needs her, loves her, and misses her.

Alpert adds an important psycho-educational piece. The husband needs to realize that the changes he sees in his wife (i.e., lack of libido) are natural and biologically based, albeit confusing, stressful, and occasionally maddening. It's not about him, not something to fight, but rather something to understand, perhaps with the help of other fathers.

In 2004 the National Marriage Project issued a statement that "children seem to be a growing impediment for the happiness of marriages." Clearly little bundles of joy can bring big boxes of unhappiness, making it urgent not to hold on to feelings of resentment and blame but to learn to discharge them in a healthy manner.

This can be done through old-fashioned communication. The objective is to reconnect rather than launch into Volume XXIII of "The Blame Game." Use "I" statements, as in, "When you kiss and coo at the baby I feel left out, like you've lost the desire to kiss me." Consider signing up for parenting classes, which offer solid tips on dealing with volatile emotions and conflicting parenting styles. Consider checking out the American Association for Marriage and Family Therapy (*www.AAMFT.org*) to find a therapist who specializes in new-parent issues.

FIELD REPORT

Having different outlooks on how to raise your kid is inevitable. We resolved those differences by agreeing on a plan for all the events we could think of, and once agreed on, sticking to it. What you don't want to do is add emotion to an already emotional situation in the moment the "crisis" is happening. It's that old boring communication-done-upfront thing. Being consistent and waiting for calm moments to go back over the plans led to less stress, a less confused kid, and more harmony in the house.

~William Babbitt, 56, Kansas City, Missouri

IF I HAD A DO-OVER

Laura Lee Carter
Fort Collins, Colorado

"Don't settle for less than you deserve."

I got married thinking it wouldn't last. Neither of us felt this was the love of our life, but we were almost forty and it was time. It wasn't a passionate relationship. I always felt like I was holding back. But in my family if you got married you had to make it work.

After seven years my husband and I just looked at each other and said, "Ewww. This really sucks." It was completely mutual. There were no kids so we just went, "You take this. I'll take that. We're done."

For a long time after the marriage I was just so depressed. Why had I compromised myself by settling for the wrong person? I had a hell of a lot of self-respect to gain.

It was really helpful to spend time alone figuring things out. I didn't run from feeling tough emotions, read great books like Gloria Steinem's *Revolution from Within*, and took walks with my dogs. . . . Most important, I contacted my college sweetheart, who had broken my heart, to finally gain closure on a relationship that had haunted me for years. Then I started a dating service. I think it was my attempt to believe in love.

I knew the minute I met Mike this was it. We talked for one hour nonstop. Four years later it still feels great between us.

Don't assume marriage has to be disappointing and that you have to compromise yourself. When you find the right person you'll know it. Have the self-respect to wait for that to happen.

CHAPTER FIVE

NOT ONE
BIG HAPPY FAMILY

A las, two people do not live in a vacuum. Dealings with extended family—in-laws, siblings—can trigger tremendous marital stress. You don't marry just your partner, but your partner's other significant others. Some of the challenges this dilemma creates for couples include figuring out boundary issues; whose needs to consider first, parents or spouse (hint: in most cases, think spouse); and being stuck for life with what you regard as a bunch of cantankerous creeps.

The questions answered by the team of marriage counselors in this chapter cut to the heart of the matter whether the pickle is an elderly, infirm mother-in-law who is ruining your life or a sister-in-law who knows much more about your life than feels comfortable.

My in-laws treat me like dirt. How can I get my wife to defend me to them?

Leanne Braddock, MEd, MA:

The undercurrent to this question is often the idea of breaking ties with the parents. However, any kind of cutoff from the in-laws will be counterproductive. Rather than say something like, "I don't want your family in our lives," he should say, "I know they're important to you but it's important for us to be on the same team."

The priority then is for the couple to work on building a more solid relationship. This involves practicing listening skills and conflict resolution. Research shows that even in the good times, we only really hear 50 percent to 75 percent of what's said to us. If we're in conflict with someone, we interpret what he or she is saying negatively. Often two to three words into a discussion a couple stops listening and starts saying invalidating things like, "I don't agree with you. That's stupid."

Instead, take turns speaking and reflect back what the other one says: "I hear that you feel demeaned by the way my parents treat you." Validate your partner by showing you understand his or her feelings. After giving each other a full hearing, brainstorm some possible tiny steps the two of you can take to begin showing a united front. It could be something along the lines of, "Every time my mother says, 'You're married to a dirt bag,' I'll say, 'I don't want to hear you speak like that about my husband.'"

In addition to defining themselves, the couple has to look hard at what they gain from the relationship with her parents. Are they counting on them for child care and/or financial help? It's a tradeoff. If the husband wants a closer relationship with his wife they might need to wind up lessening their dependence on her parents. The older couple needs to begin to see that their daughter and husband are a team.

What's happening now is the wife has divided loyalties. The key here is strengthening the marital dyad.

Elizabeth Einstein, MA/LMFT:

First the husband should ask himself why he needs his wife to defend him, and what keeps him from speaking directly to her parents.

There must be some overly close relationship between the parents and the wife, meaning she has never really separated from her parents. Thus she might not have the ego strength to tell them, "This is who I have chosen." But the husband should not ask his wife to intervene. Instead, he can deliver a clear "I" message: "I don't think you understand how hurtful it is to me when your parents do such and such. I get very frustrated."

He needs to clarify some questions: What exactly have the in-laws done to him? Does he have unrealistic expectations, maybe wanting things from them that he hasn't earned? What was his relationship like with his own parents? Did something happen to him as a child that was traumatic and now he's having a hard time discerning between perception and reality when it comes to the relationship with the in-laws?

This husband can't demand respect. He earns it. That takes time. He must stop being so insecure and do some courting. Does he spend time alone with his wife's parents? Take the father fishing? Remember the mom on her birthday separate from the daughter? That's how he develops a separate relationship versus depending on his wife to take care of things.

" MY TAKE "

Both experts agree that it's likely the wife has divided loyalties, but their comments then diverge.

While Braddock believes it permissible for the wife to stick up for her spouse to the "insulting" in-laws, Einstein demurs. The latter is firmly in the camp that the husband should fight his own battles. I agree with both. The couple should present a united front. The wife must not sit still while her parents verbally assault her life partner.

Nor should a grown man feel his place is cowering behind the apron strings of the li'l missus.

Braddock makes an interesting point vis-à-vis how many messages we miss because we're so caught up in the conversations in our head. But while the expert recommends focusing on strengthening the marital team (never a bad idea!), Einstein astutely suggests the husband look within to intuit what role his passivity and personal demons play in the way he perceives the situation. Personal responsibility is critical. In the end, the husband has to own his actions.

The first step is the united front. The next is mutually setting boundaries. For example, the word "dirt bag" should only be used in association with "vacuum cleaner"; the couple will only visit the in-laws one weekend a month rather than every Sunday; the in-laws must call before visiting versus popping in unannounced; the wife will no longer share details of marital fights with her parents. Then the pair should inform the parents together what has been decided. If the parents summarily disregard the boundaries, they need to be reminded of what is and isn't permissible—as many times as necessary.

How can I get my wife to stop telling her sister everything that goes on in our marriage?

WILLIAM J. DOHERTY, PHD:

This is a tricky one. Women tend to confide more in others about personal matters than do men. So the wife doesn't consider it a breach of trust to share intimate details of her marriage with an outsider. However, her husband feels the sharing is an invasion of privacy.

There must be boundaries. Can the couple decide, for example, that it's permissible for the wife to talk to her sister about some issues in the marriage but not others; for instance, to remain mum about their sex life? Is it touchy for the husband if his wife is sharing that he needs Viagra? That they're having trouble getting pregnant? He may be depriving his wife of some much-needed emotional support by vowing her to silence. Perhaps his standards—"I would never talk about any of this"—would be a hardship on her. However, a boundary might be too loose if after every spat she spends an hour on the phone with her sister to process the argument.

Then there is the issue of defining the sister's role. Is the conversation strictly a gripe session, with the sister agreeing the wife is blameless while giving ammunition about the totally unreasonable nature of the husband? When is this kind of conversation helpful? Is the wife getting off the phone refreshed and ready to be constructive versus returning to the marriage even more sour and self-righteous?

Another point—do the conversations stay private? Does the sister share with other family members that her brother-in-law is occasionally impotent? There has to be some confidentiality.

The two primary questions to consider here: Are the wife's boundaries fair or too loose? Is the husband trying to control his wife by setting up rules for what she can and cannot disclose to others about their private life?

Tania Paredes, LCSW, DCSW:

The wife is making the marriage secondary. She is not concerning herself with how her husband feels. She is bringing a third person into the relationship and stoking or "rehearsing" her anger toward her spouse: "Do you believe what he did to me?" If the sister is not supportive of the husband, she won't encourage the wife to work things out. Rather, she'll make her brother-in-law seem like more of a monster. It's like asking a three-time divorcée for marital advice.

The husband should ask his wife, "Why do you feel the need to put the dirty laundry out in front of your sister, especially when she is only getting your version? Why can't you talk to me about how you feel?"

It's fine to talk to a friend or sibling about intimate matters as long as there are appropriate limits and boundaries in place.

What value is there in telling the sister everything going on in the marriage?

The operational question is this: At the end of the day, are your actions affecting your marriage in a positive or negative way?

" MY TAKE "

No couple is an island—they should not be totally dependent on one another to fulfill every need. However, Paredes points out that spouses should consider themselves a team, a unit, each other's priority. Thus any confidences one spouse shares with an outsider should in some way be gauged by its potential effect on the marriage. Boundaries need to be set and honored. Dr. Doherty cautions the husband to not automatically impose his standards of privacy on his spouse. The idea is to compromise so each partner feels his or her needs are being met.

Both experts highlight the importance of defining the sister's role in the drama. If she's a fervent detractor of the brother-in-law, bringing her into the loop is akin to waving a red flag in front of a bull. The best-case scenario here is that no blood is drawn on either side.

The wife needs to ask herself why she is seeking her sister's advice. Does she need emotional support (acceptable), to vent (better to share discomfort and pain with a spouse), feel stuck and want an impartial opinion to break the deadlock à la Solomon being asked to mediate a dispute (okay, but no swords allowed), or to be proven right? If it's the latter, let her consider that if a couple's love dynamic is "I'm right/you're wrong," they both lose.

Instead of gossiping about negative events and feelings, what about occasionally bragging about something wonderful that happened (for example, the spouse got a promotion or brought home roses just because)? This way no one is betrayed and the wife is reinforcing for herself the positives about her mate and the relationship. Win-win.

I asked my widowed eighty-year-old mother-in-law to move in with us a few months ago and my life has become a living hell. Short of putting her in a nursing home, how can the situation be eased?

LEANNE BRADDOCK, MED, MA:

This is such a huge commitment. It's possible the wife felt guilted into taking this step and ended up being pretty much the sole caregiver. The couple has to share the burden. If the wife's life is a "living hell," she is probably not feeling heard or appreciated for what she is doing.

First she should tell her husband, "We need to talk about the situation with your mother. I need to let you know how I feel and I would like to hear how you feel." She might even let him go first. Chances are he also feels overwhelmed and guilty. The purpose is to give each other a "fair hearing"—one speaks and the other really listens, and then reflects back on the partner's feelings. Both people need to feel understood and validated.

Be constructive. Use "I" statements. You don't want to be accusatory and blaming; just state how you feel. "When your mother yells at me all day long I feel angry" is better than "Your mother makes me feel terrible."

Are there other siblings that might be able to contribute? Could one of them take the mother in for a period of time? Or can everyone get together and brainstorm other ideas; maybe all contribute money to allow the mother to stay in an assisted living facility?

If the couple can join forces against the problem instead of making the other the problem, the results will be more positive.

BARBARA SWENSON, PHD:

Normally I'd recommend that important decisions like, "What are we going to do if one of our parents gets sick?" be discussed ahead of time. It's usually never brought up until the situation occurs. The wife must have had some clue as to how difficult the mother-in-law would be. Did she and her husband make the decision together? That is, was the husband into opening his home as well, or was he ambivalent?

This wife needs to have a long, frank discussion about the effect his mother's living with them is having on her. Is she feeling her husband is not as supportive as he should be? We're often a lot more willing to endure trials if we feel appreciated. If he says, "We'll get Aunt Millie to stay with Mom Saturday night so you and I can go out to dinner"; he is demonstrating sensitivity to his wife's needing a break.

The main thing is the couple become a team on this problem. If they agree the mother is too demanding, they can set limits and present them to the mother. For example, if the older woman is always complaining about her daughter-in-law's cooking they can say, "We have kids and full-time jobs so four-course home-cooked meals aren't possible every day. Here's what we can and can't do." If both are steadfast, the older woman will likely accept the plan, even grudgingly.

On the flip side, the couple needs to understand what the husband's mother is going through. The aging process isn't easy. Perhaps there is a support group for senior citizens she can join where she can talk about issues like loss of autonomy. The couple can try adult day care a few days a week. It gives them a respite.

A few other thoughts: Let's say his mother won't live much longer. The couple may decide, "Well it's only six months. We'll do our best," while taking steps to deal with this major stressor in their lives. However, if the mother-in-law is this obnoxious, perhaps other living arrangements can be made?

" MY TAKE "

The consensus is this: Bring in the husband. Is the wife a silently suffering martyr? She must reach out to her spouse and make sure they are, as the lingo goes, "on the same team."

Braddock is practical and hard-boiled in her approach: Why should the couple alone have full responsibility for the difficult elder foisted upon them? Share the pain.

Dr. Swenson adds the empathy factor: Walk a mile in the mother-in-law's shoes. I love her suggestion of looking for ways to make the elderly woman less unhappy. If her needs and longings are considered and an effort made to assuage her loneliness she will likely stop making the lives of everyone around her "a living hell." On the plus side, if the stars are aligned, the relative is at death's door and will soon be exiting feet-first!

Along with being a team and setting limits with their house-guest, the couple can bring in a geriatric social worker to offer suggestions, speak with the elderly woman, and provide information about possible services and benefits to which they may be entitled and that would make their lives a bit easier.

My wife's ex is constantly making excuses to spend time with her. We have a really good marriage. She swears there's nothing to be jealous of. But if that's the truth, why won't she tell him to bug off? Shouldn't my feelings be more important than his?

Elizabeth Einstein, MA/LMFT:

I would have lots of questions. How long ago was the divorce? Did she remarry too soon after splitting up with her former partner? She may not have emotionally resolved the divorce. I have several clients who share the same complaint. Part of the problem is that some women are not assertive. Perhaps she was with an alcoholic or abusive spouse with whom she was passive, and the pattern continues. Maybe she didn't take the time between marriages to strengthen herself but was looking for someone to care for her emotionally and economically. The decision was made on an unconscious level but can set up a dynamic like the one described.

Another possible reason for this situation might be that she has children with her former husband and fears if she doesn't attempt to keep him happy, he may take it out on the kids; for instance, by being verbally abusive to them. So this wife may be trying to play it both ways.

My other question is, if things are truly resolved with her ex and says there is nothing for the husband to worry about, why is he so insecure? If she has children from the former marriage and he doesn't have any, it's possible that this husband doesn't have an understanding of the powerful bond between a wife and her offspring.

RENÉE A. COHEN, PHD:

The husband needs to address this issue with his wife at a neutral time, meaning not just after she's seen her ex. This way he can come across in an unemotional and non-accusatory way, using "I" statements: "I know you say there's nothing going on between the two of you, but I'm confused about why you see him."

He needs to keep posing questions to help both of them get a better understanding of what's going on. Hopefully during the exploration a light bulb will go off. Depending on how the relationship ended, the wife may feel guilty and obliged to do what the ex asks. Or she might like additional attention from a man; seeing her husband jealous reinforces the notion that he loves her. Nobody engages in a relationship that doesn't benefit him or her; hence the need for the exploration, which will hopefully give her some insight as to how seeing her ex benefits her.

The second part the husband needs to convey to his wife is that he finds this association painful: "I don't know if you know it, but it really hurts me that you see him." Again, you don't want to make the other person feel defensive. The goal is clarification.

If children are involved there needs to be a continuation of the relationship with the ex, but if that is not the case, at some point you need closure. It's up to the wife to prioritize and to realize her actions are hurtful to her husband. She may have been so involved in her needs that she didn't realize her husband felt diminished in some fashion. She needs to consider how her behavior affects her husband, his feelings, and ultimately their relationship.

What is most important to her? If it's to maintain a relationship with her ex, that speaks volumes! If it's to make her husband feel safe, she needs to make him her priority. If she feels something is lacking in her marriage, she might tell her husband: "When I see my ex he compliments me. That makes me feel pretty." The husband can then say, "Oh, I didn't realize you needed that." There has to be an awareness of something amiss, an acknowledgment something must be done.

This couple has a chance to expand the base of their relationship, to be honest with each other and to really understand there are three components to a marriage—him, her, and the relationship. At all times they must be aware of all three elements.

" MY TAKE "

This is a touchy scenario, one that can test a marriage. Both experts offer sensible, helpful advice. Einstein points out that many women have trouble saying no, consequently allowing themselves to be manipulated into a situation that is outside their best interest. However, as Einstein also brings out, if the marriage is a sound one, the husband needs to explore the roots of his jealousy. Doubtless his insecurities didn't begin with this situation, or even with this relationship. It is historic; detritus from childhood.

Dr. Cohen emphasizes the importance of honest and noncensuring communication. Of particular note is her emphasis on communication with the goal of clarification for both partners. Just as the wife must consider that she might be putting her needs ahead of the needs of the entity known as "the marriage," the husband must recognize why his partner desires this outside stimulation. What is he not giving her that she craves?

Both experts stress that if children are involved, the father will never be out of the picture. But that doesn't mean reasonable boundaries cannot be established for ongoing contact between the exes.

While I greatly respect the opinions of Einstein and Dr. Cohen, and agree that the two exes should not be bosom buddies (platonically speaking), I do want to present another perspective.

If the marriage is solid, and thus the friendship no threat, the wife might feel the husband's jealousy bespeaks a grievous lack of trust and respect for her. When two people are married, they share a life together. When that shared life ends—so long as the parting is not acrimonious—does that mean the parties should stop caring about one another, cease and desist even in a casual way keeping track of one another's lives?

Again, I am not suggesting the ex be a major part of his former wife's life—no intimate dinner dates or runs in the park—but the current husband should at least make an effort to understand that the wife might truly be making a sacrifice by choosing to respect his wishes. It will sting a little. What can he do for her to assuage her pain and make her feel loved and nurtured above all?

I hate his family. My husband and they are very close. We see them every weekend. What can I do to get out of seeing them so often?

REBECCA ROY, MA, MFT:

My best advice is to cultivate a sense of humor. With that in place you can tolerate almost anyone's annoying habits.

Negotiate with your husband. For instance, suggest he continue visiting his family every weekend, while you join him every other weekend. Or keep making up excuses to get out of seeing them. But eventually, particularly around the holidays, you'll have to tolerate them. Find techniques to keep from being drawn into uncomfortable situations.

Recognize that you can't control anyone's behavior but your own. Try to observe these people's actions without judgment. For instance, say your mother-in-law is very controlling. You don't have to respond. Say to yourself, "Okay, she's trying to get to me but I have choices. I don't have to get agitated or angry. She might escalate her outrageous behavior but I don't have to escalate with her."

The point is that rather than getting pulled in, you can step back and watch it all. Get a feel for what's going on. Sometimes several family members try to pull you in, asking you to pick sides: "Don't you think that so and so is wrong?" This is dangerous territory. Avoid it at all costs. Respond, "It's not my place to say who's right or wrong."

Your husband is in a tough position. You may not always have him on your side. It's up to you to protect your emotional well-being. However, while it's not your husband's job to manage your emotional responses, he should offer understanding and empathy. Talk to him about what you are doing: "My tactic with your family is to keep a neutral stance." If you're really desperate, bring a friend along. Hopefully, the family won't behave badly in front of outsiders.

BEVERLY SMALLWOOD, PhD:

"I hate his family." That's quite a blanket statement. Every member of his family? There's nothing remotely positive about any one of them? Any time I hear a person generalizing an intensely negative label about an entire group, or even one person, I work with them on the possibility that they have seen some things they don't like, then assumed that everything about each person is despicable. I would challenge you to examine your perceptions to see if any of these are true:

- You are blaming all your husband's faults on them.
- You are assuming that their differences from your own family are automatically bad.
- You find interactions unpleasant—does that mean you have to hate them?

You are choosing to be with your husband, so to some degree his family is part of your reality. To say or imply to him that his family is terrible is in a sense to say that he is defective. So at least a part of the solution has to be working on your attitude and approach to them. This might be tough, but I do know that it does not facilitate communication and goodwill to be steaming inside whenever you are around them. Can you find the person or persons in the family who are the least offensive to you and make a positive gesture—for example, a considerate act, a cup of coffee—to try to bring some of those walls down?

That being said, if you and your husband are spending an inordinate amount of time with his family, it's perfectly okay to set boundaries on that. Talk with your husband without any major put-downs of his family, which will only make him defensive and resistant to your requests. Tell him, "I understand that your family is important to you. True, I don't see eye-to-eye with them on many things, but I know that you want to spend time with them—more time than I do, though I'm not saying I won't be with them some. However, I'm also concerned about our own family. It's really important to me that we have enough of our own times together. What suggestions do you have for us working this out?" Have some suggestions for compromise in your back pocket.

Extended families can be challenging, that's the truth. However, they come with the territory of the person you love. X-ing them out is probably not an option. Combine empathy for your husband, a courageous challenge to your own attitudes, and a determination to work out a plan that works for you and your spouse.

" MY TAKE "

The short answer according to the experts queried here is that this woman cannot just push a button and cause the hated relatives to slide down a chute, vanishing forevermore. For the sake of her husband she's got to find some way to broker a détente.

Roy's suggestion that the letter-writer learn to monitor her emotions and not become drawn into battle is an admirable one. To further that aim, the wife might study meditation with its focus on becoming centered, in the moment, not reactive or "attached" to getting her way. However, I strongly disagree with the therapist's half-facetious comment that bringing a friend along as a human shield has merit. Some "battles" are best waged alone . . . or with the help of a spouse. Thus I take issue with Roy's assertion that the husband isn't someone the wife can turn to for alliance. It's true he should not be put in the middle and that the wife must respect his familial ties. However, if his "for better for worse" partner is indeed being put in a painfully awkward situation by his other nearest and dearest he can offer up to the folks, "Please don't put Charlotte in the middle of your fight. That's been going on for decades and has nothing to do with her." Spouses need to protect one another under sniper fire.

Dr. Smallwood's aim is to sharpen the vision of the psychologically myopic that refuse or are unable to see their role in the hostilities. Honest self-reflection allows for the possibility of reappraising a situation and looking for new solutions. While the therapist doesn't downplay the challenges of dealing with difficult relatives and is on board with the idea of setting rules and boundaries, her sharp advice is geared toward the direction of compromise.

I am curious what this woman's relationship is like with her own family. Perhaps conflict-ridden, tumultuous, and isolating, and being with them made her feel like an alien? Meeting her husband, she hoped she'd found someone with whom to form a tight-knit unit of two. But instead her spouse wanted her to spend more than a little time with his nuclear family. Alas, being with them triggers the discomfort and sense of alienation that is in some ways her default setting—painful but something that feels familiar.

A wife in this position should ask the husband why he enjoys spending so much time with his family, what it feels like being with them. She should share her own experiences growing up. Then, being careful not to attack his loved ones, she should share how being around his family makes her feel now. Then the couple can work together when attending family gatherings to ensure the wife feels included and accepted as much as possible.

FIELD REPORT

Last year my husband and I had a rift with his mother right before Mother's Day. We didn't talk to her for several months. Being willing to walk away tends to have an effect. She wound up apologizing. Now for the sake of a healthy relationship we all say what's on our mind and everybody's getting along. Communication is key.

~ Patty Mooney, 53, San Diego, California

FROM THE FILES OF . . .

Cloé Madanes, PhD, FAPA

Dr. Madanes recaps: "A woman called me, crying desperately. She and her husband had been married thirty-nine years. During that time there had been two separations. They had three adult children and ran a hotel together. The wife said there was no communication."

The therapist continues, "When they came into my office I said to the husband, 'I talked to your wife a little. Let me hear from you.' He enthusiastically talked about growing up on a farm. After a while I said to the wife, "You said there was a communication problem. He seems very communicative. What's the problem?"

The wife cried, "He doesn't communicate with me. He's not interested in me."

Dr. Madanes ordered, "Give me an example of something really traumatic he did."

The woman recalled a bus tour in Europe the pair had taken together. She told the counselor, "He looked out the window, or if there was nothing to see, read a book instead of talking to me."

When quizzed if she'd asked what the book was about, the answer was no. The next comment from the therapist: "Maybe you can ask him now."

The book was about bridges, a topic of great interest to the husband. He said to his wife, "I would have loved to talk to you about it but you didn't seem interested."

Dr. Madanes asked the wife what did interest her. The wife said, "Spirituality. I love attending Deepak Chopra's conferences, but that doesn't interest my husband."

The therapist commented, "I don't blame him. Those conferences can be boring. But he is interested in bridges." She then asked the husband if he would enjoy discussing current events with his wife. He answered, "I'd love that. But it doesn't interest her."

Dr. Madanes explains, "This is the type of couple between whom it's necessary to create a bridge. Each person has to get more interested in what interests the other."

This is accomplished by opening one's mind and heart rather than maintaining a self-righteous way of viewing the world. Says Dr. Madanes, "This couple ultimately made that bridge and improved their communication. They came to understand the importance of asking each other the right questions about what interested the other."

They also learned to capitalize on their common interests—the children, the hotel they worked closely together to run.

Their sex life improved as well. The wife initially kept stating, "He's not attracted to me." The husband's response was, "She's gorgeous! I've just given up after being turned away so many times." Dr. Madanes's advice to the wife: "Attack him at least once a week. Take him completely by surprise and see what power you have as a woman!"

The therapy worked beautifully and the couple is closer than at any point in their marriage.

Dr. Madanes explains, "Couples come to me from all over the world nursing hurt feelings for years on end about things that are ridiculous. For instance, this wife was brooding about her husband reading a book on a bus. Meanwhile it didn't occur to her to ask him anything about it. People have to accept that their mate is different, accept the playfulness that can come from the differences between the sexes, and accept that each has a bit of a dark side. No one is perfect."

If a couple can loosen up and recognize one another's imperfections they will be well on the way to creating a marriage built to withstand anything!

CHAPTER SIX

HAVE SOME FAITH

—————— ✥ ——————

Faith is a ferociously individual concept, something personal, even primal. Thus it can have a huge impact on a marriage regardless of whether the urgent issue is negotiating an interfaith relationship when children are involved or pondering whether it's possible for a couple to forge a cosmic connection. The specificity of these issues called for a particularly astute array of marital experts including Harville Hendrix, PhD, cofounder of Imago Relationship, a couples therapy he developed with his wife.

In this chapter you'll find savvy and sensitive advice on dilemmas ranging from helping a wife break it to her husband that she wants to renege on an agreement they made years back about the religion in which they would raise their daughter to opening a dialogue between a couple who share the same religion but differ drastically on just how to practice their faith.

My husband and I are both Jewish but I'm not observant and resent staying home every Friday night. How can we learn to accommodate each other's beliefs?

SHARON M. RIVKIN, MA, MFT:

Despite the anger and resentment that has likely built up, the wife needs to approach her partner in a way that does not make him defensive. For example, if she says, "I don't want to stay home Friday night," the husband won't budge. If she instead says, "I really understand how important observing the holiday is to you. I don't want to offend or undermine, but I'm not in the same place. We need to talk about agreeing to disagree and come up with some compromise," there's an opening.

When someone isn't defensive, all sorts of interesting things come out. Knowing our partner cares makes us willing to go a long way. Perhaps the agreement can be the wife stays home just one or two Friday nights of the month. Or she can go out on Friday night but remain at home all day Saturday with her husband.

If the spouse has a very rigid belief, it's harder to negotiate. He might not be able to bend at all. Some counseling might be necessary. However, it's worth a try for the wife not to attack but to admit, "I'm getting angry." Maybe he can then say, "I'd like you home with me but I guess I can live with you going out every other Friday night." If his position is set in stone, she has to decide if it's worth it to keep resisting. She can also look at why she married him, knowing about his rigidity.

It never hurts to open a dialogue. Even when there is a disagreement, as long as there is openness and sharing, a moment of intimacy can develop. The wife can pretend she's talking to a stranger. People are usually nicer to strangers than to their mates. When her partner was a stranger, she was likely really interested in him! She should go back to that time, invite her husband in, being curious instead of assuming she knows everything about him. And if both people need to be right all the time, no one wins.

Marion Solomon, PhD:

In a situation like this I suggest couples ask themselves: "On a scale of one to ten, how important is this issue to me?" If something is a ten for your partner and a three for you, go with your partner. He needs to side with you when the scale of importance is reversed. This is about reciprocity. Ask yourself, "Is it really important I get this? Will it end the relationship if I say no to what my spouse wants?"

Pay attention to what is more important—maintaining the relationship or having Friday nights free. Is every issue a ten, meaning you can never budge on what you want? I've worked with couples where an argument about which restaurant to go to for dinner becomes a big issue. Then what route to take to the restaurant becomes a big issue. That means what is important here is: Who gets to do what? This is about who has control in the relationship.

" MY TAKE "

The bottom line here is voiced by Dr. Solomon: What's more important, the relationship or going out on Friday nights? Or it could be asked this way: What's more important, the relationship or insisting your partner never goes out Friday nights? The expert's point is that a person can be so blinded by the need for control that he or she loses sight of what's healthy for the relationship.

Rivkin also touches on the "needing to be right" peril, which can cause a communication lockdown. It's dangerous for the relationship when one or both partners are rigid, not just when it comes to the importance of maintaining a certain lifestyle but in how each views the other's personality and belief systems. I like the therapist's comment about treating one's spouse as one would a stranger—with an open mind and the forbearance not to jump in and interrupt every five seconds.

Rivkin brings up another interesting point. Didn't the wife know beforehand that her husband had a very strong view of how religion should be observed? People tend to marry someone who will bring out some childhood issue, then keep batting their heads against that same hard wall. In this wife's case, perhaps her opinion was never taken seriously by her parents.

A "mixed" marriage between a religious and secular mate has its share of potential pitfalls. A 1996 study of married couples by Israeli sociologists Leonard and Sonia Weller found that the Sabbath causes conflict—for instance, secular spouses want to go to the beach, take a drive, and so on. Compromises in these "intra-marriages" fell into three basic types. Five couples practiced "separate but equal" lifestyles wherein the non-religious spouse behaved in public and at home just as he or she did before the marriage. Thirteen couples settled on a solution involving the nonobservant spouse observing religious laws in public but behaving in a secular fashion at home. Among the remaining eleven couples, one spouse adopted the other's lifestyle—five religious spouses becoming non-observant and six secular spouses becoming religious.

What this shows is that it's important to be creative and flexible. Each person, whether religious or not, must treat his or her partner's needs not with derision but as something holy and sacred. Love thy partner as thou love thyself!

How can I get my wife to accept that I'm not spiritually bankrupt just because I don't believe in God?

RABBI YEHUDA BERG:

According to Kabbalah we don't have to believe in a God, but we do need to believe in some type of cause and effect, some spiritual system. So if you believe that the world isn't random, that's enough for me, spiritually speaking, even if for you there's no figurehead on top. You shouldn't be judged. Sharing brings out positive energy. Insisting the other believe as you do brings out negative energy.

Someone who is religiously dogmatic needs to believe a certain way. What a couple should strive for is open dialogue. They should understand that simply going to church or temple doesn't make a person spiritual. Is this a deal breaker—"Come to temple with me or else"? Try to do something spiritual together, like taking a class. It's about trying to build bridges.

PAUL DUNION, EdD, LPC:

This couple is experiencing a conflict of values. Each has a different belief. Often this diversity leads to someone feeling threatened: I was counting on you to reinforce my values! How can there be so much difference between us?

When there is an unmet need, couples typically go into one of three postures. These postures are primitive defenses that are centered in the front brain or lower right brain, where it feels like "fight or flight." Common as these postures are, none are constructive. The first posture is attempting to distance. The person pulls away emotionally and/or physically. The second posture is attempting to influence the other's opinion by becoming self-righteous. For instance, the husband in this scenario might give his wife three reasons why she's an idiot not to see his point of view. The third posture is to be adaptive to the other person's position. This means he actually takes on the belief system, values, or desires of his partner. There is a significant loss of individuality.

Once we can begin to own our defensive actions and diminish the level of blame and accusation, we can begin building a rapport with our partner. This involves asking yourself, "Am I open at all to learning from my spouse?" That's when you move into the frontal lobe of the brain, where it's possible to generate creative options together. The fourth option for handling a values diversity issue then becomes exploring self-accountability together. When a problem arises, the couple recognizes that it stems from an unmet need as opposed to seeing each other as unloving.

In twenty-seven years of working with couples I've usually found that unmet needs fall into two expressions—wanting either more connection or more autonomy. The former need almost automatically is ascribed to woman and the latter to men. That's an illusion! However, those two needs are always operating in a relationship.

Once there is self-accountability the problem is not seen as wrong or bad and there is no need to be defensive. If each can let go of the need to influence the other person and rather learn from his or her partner's viewpoint, the couple can get creative and resilient at dealing with different values.

" MY TAKE "

Rabbi Berg and Dr. Dunion offer intriguing takes on how to handle this spiritual divide. Rabbi Berg stresses that being dogmatic and insistent that one's partner behave in a very narrow manner is not good for marriages, much less peace talks between warring nations. Both causes are better served by putting out positive energy, building bridges, negotiating land demarcations. But I digress.

Dr. Dunion likens this dilemma to a clash of differing values. He says couples often handle such clashes by feeling threatened and reacting primitively, i.e., being self-righteous. The solution involves developing an awareness of our deeply ingrained patterns, "owning" our bad behavior and moving into a different part of our brain. He echoes the futility-of-being-rigid thesis offered by Rabbi Berg. Dead ends can morph into open roads once couples, as my mother used to put it, stop banging their heads against the wall and move slightly to the right or left.

Kahlil Gibran said, "Love is the offspring of spiritual affinity." In this context spiritual affinity is defined as a common way of viewing the world. It is a spark that unites people when they meet, giving them that little frisson of, "Yippee! Someone gets me. I am not the only one who sees things in this particular way." To forge a spiritual union, the bedrock belief must be faith in the marriage. When that is a given, the partners should be open and trusting enough to allow each other to be true to himself or herself versus being threatened by certain disharmonious beliefs—for instance, only one spouse believes in the Big Kahuna.

I fervently believe religion and spirituality are often confused. This is where the dogma comes in. If one partner hangs over the other a non-spiritual judgment—"You are not a good enough person if you don't worship God the way I do"—it's not according the partner respect.

However, if the practice of religion is very important to one partner and not to another, especially when there are children involved, the skills of empathy and compromise are crucial. Be supportive of a partner lighting the Sabbath candles. Don't denigrate if your mate isn't a churchgoer. But always, always worship at the altar of the relationship. Amen.

How can I tell my husband that now that our daughter is school age, I've decided I'm not comfortable raising her in both our faiths? The religious traditions I was raised with mean more to me than I realized.

MARY HAMMOND, MA:

Rather than give answers, I prefer the couple explore what their own solution might be. I'd want the wife to talk about why she's changed her mind. What occurred that caused her to go more deeply into her religion? Several years back she'd made an agreement out of love for her husband that wasn't authentic for her. Or perhaps as time passed she began to see that their child couldn't handle the dichotomy of being involved in two religions.

I'd also want to know more about the marriage. Is this disagreement over how to raise the child truly the core issue or symptomatic of other conflicts? Good communication helps in discussing areas of conflict. I'd want the wife to preface talk of the problem with an emotional disclaimer: "This may be hard for you to hear. I know we had an agreement about raising Suzie in both our faiths but it's not working for me anymore. I'm not sure where you stand." The spouse can then add something like: "I'd like to have a discussion about our spirituality." The idea is to open a dialogue versus issuing an ultimatum.

The way this dialogue should occur is via reflective listening. One person speaks, followed by the other reflecting back the content and the feelings underneath. This husband could say: "Even though you said you wanted to raise our child in both faiths now you feel this would be too confusing for her." When the wife feels heard, truly understood, her spouse gets a turn to talk about his feelings. She listens in turn and reflects back.

Problem-solving is the next step. This involves brainstorming, getting all the possibilities on the table without nay-saying any of them no matter how outrageous some may seem. When the possibilities are exhausted the couple can take them one by one and have a discussion to hopefully reach a happy medium. For instance, perhaps they'll decide to go primarily to the wife's church but observe some of the holidays surrounding the husband's faith.

JAY P. GRANAT, PHD:

People are allowed to change their minds, though I'd be curious to learn what caused the shift in the wife's feelings. Was there some experience she underwent that was revelatory? The wife's beliefs need to be respected.

Is there a compromise? I'd ask each person, "What's your comfort zone around this? Where can you be if not 100 percent happy, at least eighty-five percent?" Perhaps the couple and their daughter can sit down as a family. The girl is young and at this point may or may not want to go for some kind of religious training. But she can be part of the discussion.

When couples are not rigid—my way or the highway!—creative ideas can emerge. One couple, a Jew and a Protestant, wound up doing extensive research and ultimately became Buddhist. Another couple decided to send their six-year-old to religious school for two years, after which period they reassessed how this lifestyle was working out.

In some cases a spouse brings up something this provocative to create a battleground, perhaps an an excuse to get out of the marriage. That kind of scenario can lead to the couple going to court.

" MY TAKE "

As Dr. Granat points out, people are allowed to change their minds. Nothing is static. Growth is wonderful, although it can prove challenging for a marriage when one partner changes and the other doesn't. But if the wife can be expressive and open and the husband curious about his mate's new position rather than defensive and combative (granted, this can be a tall order when a status quo is threatened), it can help the couple reach a compromise that is acceptable to all parties. However, I question how much input a child can or should have at this stage: "Hey cutie? Which church or temple are you interested in going to? I'll give you an ice cream cone if you choose mine."

Hammond joins Dr. Granat in suggesting that communication is essential here, with an emphasis on reflective listening without judgment, followed by a period of brainstorming. Dialoguing, not issuing ultimatums, is what can ultimately bring this touchy problem to a compromise.

While not quite in the same sphere as discovering you were cheated on, the spouse whose status quo was rocked might for a time feel betrayed. He or she is entitled to voice those feelings—not to dwell, but in an effort to get past the bitterness and move on. This is where having a good support system comes in handy, as you don't want to keep unloading on your mate, who has not set out to hurt you but rather experienced a spiritual metamorphosis.

It's also helpful for interfaith couples even at this "late" stage of their relationship to share memories and feelings about their childhood religious celebrations and practices and what elements they most wish to impart to their child. For instance, even if the child is raised Jewish, the Christian partner can still create rituals with the youngster, perhaps placing beloved holiday ornaments in a prominent spot and describing the meaning of each.

It's our first Christmas/Hanukkah as a married couple. How can we please both sets of parents, who each expect us to be with them on the holidays and celebrate their traditions?

SHEILA BENDER, PHD:

Each of you has a vast history of what the holidays mean to you. Often couples don't talk about these things. Rather, they carry expectations based on their experiences. They become narrow in their thinking process—"This is how it's always been. This is how it always has to be."—rather than expansive. They need to talk about their feelings and also think about ways to enlarge the experience. Perhaps the wife's mother is widowed. Rather than expect her daughter and son-in-law to come visit, she might be open to attending a bigger party with her son-in-law's family even if they celebrate different traditions.

Thus communication is important. But so is developing a sense that you are no longer just part of your birth families but together comprise a new one. There needs to be a splitting off from both sets of parents. A popular solution is to go to one set of parents one year, and the other one the next. Or during the same year spend Christmas Eve at one house and Christmas Day at another.

RABBI YEHUDA BERG:

Focus on being together. After all, the holidays come once a year and comprise approximately a ten-day period. It shouldn't negatively impact the next 355 days. Use this as an opportunity to grow together. Don't go into your separate bunkers. Create a challenge: "What would be more difficult for us to do as a couple?" Crazy relatives bring out difficult issues that need to be worked on.

It's not just, "Where do we go for dinner?" It's about conflicts that have come about with your family because you married a Catholic girl. This dilemma needs to be put on the table and discussed: "My mother can't understand why I did this but I'm not going to let that come between us." Setting these rules helps you navigate through the challenges. There might not be an ideal solution, but work through it all together.

" MY TAKE "

Dr. Bender and Rabbi Berg offer solid advice for couples caught on the horns of what is often referred to as the "December Dilemma."

Dr. Bender's comment about how deeply a person's personal history impacts him or her, setting up often unspoken expectations of exactly the way the holidays should be spent, is a crucial one. Instead of holding on to a rigid definition of what a proper celebration should entail, brainstorm together to create some unique traditions that will begin to define the new family as a unit. While I applaud the concept of looking for ways to enlarge the experience, don't be too surprised if the wife's single mother remains locked into her wish to spend the holidays at home with her daughter dancing attendance!

In answer to the Rabbi's point, crazy relatives bring up lots of tough issues and unsettling feelings. Yes, it's good training to view these problems as something to solve together. But since holidays can be hard to get through in the best of times, perhaps couples can cut themselves a break and choose the second-most difficult challenge to tackle.

According to the American Jewish Committee, about 750,000 people are in Jewish-Christian relationships. Of those, many face the sometimes epic "how do we please the parents?" trauma. The best course is to "train" the folks to realize that they are no longer boss. The experts rightly stress the importance of the couple communicating with one other. But they shouldn't back away from communicating with the parents. This involves telling the parents (without the spouse present) that while they will always be loved, honored, and an important priority, they are no longer the most important one. The marriage has to come first. Listen to their feelings—indeed, encourage them to express what's on their minds—but also voice the hope that in the spirit of the holidays the parents will accept the new order.

It's also important to inform the parents that if they still harbor resentment they should bring it to their child. Bringing it to their daughter- or son-in-law would be counterproductive, not helpful to the goal of having everyone get along.

Afterward, let the spouse know the gist of this conversation and ask him or her to let you know if the in-laws persist in making awkward remarks and demands. Again, each spouse must be the point person for touchy conversations with his or her own family. Additionally, each spouse must respect the in-laws' traditions. For instance, call to say Merry Christmas and wrap their presents in gay Santa wrappings even if you don't celebrate that holiday.

Once the boundaries are established, it becomes easier over time to chart this new territory, relating to both sets of parents with mutual respect and goodwill.

My partner of eight years and I love one another but I envy couples who seem spiritually connected. Is it possible at this stage of the game to transform our relationship?

HARVILLE HENDRIX, PHD:

Make a decision to surrender all negativity toward your partner, meaning stop thinking of him or her as in some way not as good as you. A "judgmental mind" causes one spouse to criticize another via shame, blame, guilt, deflection, put-downs, etc. The negativity is due to anxiety. There is something about your mate's "otherness," the different viewpoint, that you see as threatening. But when you are judging or devaluing someone you cannot feel connected.

This devaluing can be over something big, like making a major decision without first consulting you, or about something small, like being late. Maybe you have abandonment issues from childhood or are obsessive compulsive so your partner's keeping you waiting fifteen minutes can set off your judgmental mind. People don't always stop to think about the psychological mechanisms that underlie their feelings and behaviors.

To nourish rather than rupture a connection you must activate an "accepting mind" that views your partner as simply different from you. This mindset starts with being curious. You could say, "Oh, you're late. What happened?" Let him or her answer, then mirror back accurately and without judgment or distortion what you hear: "You didn't mean to leave me waiting, but your boss called you in for a meeting you couldn't get out of." This allows you to move into empathy. Perhaps your partner is very worried about job security and thus saw no choice but to stay late at work. While this is not your internal world, you can now better understand how it is your partner's. Understanding the feelings driving the behavior causes you to become empathic about an action that earlier angered you.

Recent scientific studies have revealed that empathy triggers the same part of the brain as meditation. Empathy offers communion. It is in those moments that a deep connection occurs. This process of being available, truly listening to and mirroring your partner, requires becoming centered and quiet inside. It is a spiritual practice.

Pat Love, EdD:

A couple striving to form a more connected bond should sit together, close their eyes, and remember a time they felt so spiritually connected it was as if they made up one person. They should make an effort to remember every single detail—the thoughts, smells, tastes, feelings. They should open their eyes and take turns sharing the experience and what it was like: "Remember that time at Lake Tahoe when we sat by the lake and even though the cars were whizzing by you took my hand?" By being able to recall these moments they learn that experiencing them again is possible.

To be truly connected requires slowing things down. You can't be intimate and attuned to one another when you're multitasking. To have a "mindful" marriage you must give your full attention to your partner. Focus on being in his presence; concentrate on the feel of her body, the smell of her hair.

The biggest deterrent is lack of attunement. Approximately 80 percent of couples who divorce say they grew apart. You have to be your partner's priority. When you withdraw your energy it leaves a void. Want your mate's attention? Just focus your attention on him or her.

It is possible to discuss a wonderful, connected time the two of you shared without verbally beating your partner over the head with it. A woman wants to talk and talk, but too much talking takes her husband out of the intimacy.

My definition of spirituality is anything that connects you to your higher power. When you can tune out the world and tune in to your partner you are connecting to his or her higher power. Honor each other with your full presence and you will feel as one.

" MY TAKE "

Boiled down, the advice here is simple yet profound: To feel as one, stop focusing on one—yours truly.

Granted, this is not an easy task, but the less one is ruled by unconscious, childhood-mired needs, the easier it is to view the life partner as a unique and amazing, if flawed, individual, not as someone put on the earth solely to be a great spouse. Genuine connection requires a slowing down, muting the noise in one's head.

Dr. Hendrix points out that one partner judging another can lead to unhappiness and frustration for both. Empathizing with the other person allows for both to be, as Dr. Love puts it, fully present in the moment.

When one is standing atop a diving board staring twenty feet down there is often a hesitancy to jump in, despite knowing intellectually that the pool underneath is full.

It can feel like the same leap of faith when contemplating opening up and confiding those innermost, sometimes shameful secrets. Make the jump; stop hiding, and get emotionally naked (much harder than physically naked!) in front of the most important person in the world. And when he or she is brave enough to do a soul-level striptease, reward it with respect, honor, love, and gentleness.

On a crucial level, spiritual union is based on being both trusting and trustworthy.

FIELD REPORT

I'm Catholic and my husband is Jewish. We dated for six years with no problems from our families, but once we got engaged in 1988, all hell broke lose. I wanted an interfaith ceremony and my in-laws went around looking like they were going to a funeral. We ended up just having a judge, and the ceremony was two seconds long. This cast a pall over the first few years of marriage for me. But I don't believe in holding a grudge. It's unproductive to be mad at people. We get along fine now.

~Christina Gombar, 49, Saunderstown, Rhode Island

LASTING LOVE

Florence and Jim Harris
Boston, Massachusetts, married 40 years

"It's not the marriage I envisioned for myself."

Married forty years, when Florence and Jim met the odds were small they'd make it to a second date.

The pair met at grad school in Boston. "There was an instant physical attraction," Florence explains, adding, "but so many important factors weren't right that a relationship seemed impossible."

For one thing, Florence was dating someone who lived in another city—someone "appropriate," as in sharing her religion (Jewish). This other person also shared her desire to live a comfortable urban lifestyle, preferably in New York.

"Then there was me," laughs Jim, "Baptist and an academic who would never make much money."

"Not my cup of tea," Florence admits.

It didn't help that both sets of parents were adamantly opposed to the match.

After a year the pair stopped dating and Florence tried to work things out with Mr. Appropriate. But she couldn't get Jim out of her head . . . or heart.

Eight months later they reconnected. "We agonized and agonized—sometimes it just seemed impossible. . . ."

Jim finishes her sentence: "But we found each other irresistible."

There were compromises. Jim converted ("I was already nonpracticing, so it wasn't a wrenching business"). And Florence agreed to be the wife of a professor at MIT whose only shot at striking it rich was an errant Lotto ticket.

Once they wed, it never occurred to either of them they would ever un-wed.

"There are many things I'd like to change about my husband, but I've never wanted to change husbands."

"She would like me to be handsome and not so neat," Jim says.

And he would love her to be neater and more of a homebody.

"You do things that aren't important to you but they are to the other person," Florence says, adding, "I learned how to cook and clean the house to make him happy."

Happily, their basic set of values—the make-or-break issues—were compatible. Both wanted marriage, children, . . . and a dog. "If he didn't like animals or music or was a Republican, now that would have been a problem!" Florence says fiercely.

Yes, deciding to marry was scary. Staying married is easy.

"Couples can get very angry and have real conflict, but you have to accept the fact that you're different and there will be bad times. . . ."

Florence finishes for her husband: "But there is something deeper that holds you together and that's the glue."

They're silent, thinking. Jim admits, "There was a bit of midlife crisis, but you just become forty-one and forty-two and keep going. It's the way our parents were and that's our style as well."

Florence says, "He has his foibles, little crazy-making things, but that makes him interesting."

In the end, the big secret to their relationship is that there is no secret. Once they took that stumbling journey to "I do," they just did—forever.

"We really respect each other," Florence finishes with a touch of earnestness. "Even when we mock each other's weaknesses, it's done with love."

CHAPTER SEVEN

INFIDELITY:
END OF THE ROAD?

I n a society where 41 percent of marriages involve a confession of infidelity, it is clear there is an urgent need for
couples to find effective ways to grapple with the underlying causes of faithlessness, as well as complexities such as
whether the guilty party should confess and how the aftermath of the affair can become a healing experience. In this
chapter John Gray, PhD, is one of the gifted therapists offering advice on dilemmas ranging from whether to confess to a
one-night stand to what culpability for an affair the "cheated-
on" partner possesses.

I had a one-night stand while on a business trip. I used protection and will never see this person again, but guilt is eating at me. Should I tell my spouse?

Gay Hendricks, PhD, and Kathlyn Hendricks, PhD, ADTR:

Yes; otherwise, instead of having a relationship with your spouse you have one with your secrets. We've seen thousands of couples who've faced this situation find that their marriage subsequently flourishes.

What most people are trying to avoid by not telling is the inconvenience of the other person's reaction. They don't want to experience their partner's hurt and disappointment and so choose secrecy. But when you tell the truth you actually create an opportunity in the marriage. It doesn't matter what the "truth" is about. What matters is that you say something that is true for you.

If you're concerned the other person really doesn't want to know, ask, "With regard to really important things, would you rather I tell the truth or lie to you?" If she says "I'd rather be lied to," follow that path. But if you hear something like, "I'm committed to you being totally honest with me. That's more important than preserving my illusions or worrying about hurting my feelings," that's your answer.

Broach the incident in a ten-second conversation: "I had a one-night stand with Sally Smith Thursday night and I feel terrible." Leave room for your partner to express what's true for her. Be willing to listen.

An aspect of telling the truth is that it opens up a new level of intimacy. Passion for the marriage can be rediscovered. It's bucking up and pushing through something uncomfortable. It's actually sexy, an aphrodisiac. When both people realize they've been conspiring by not acknowledging problems in the marriage, by having an unconscious decision to remain ignorant, finally being honest can help bridge the gulf. It's also a way for both people to take responsibility rather than letting one partner be the bad guy. When you can see the affair was a symptom and that being able to discuss it is a gateway to being real with one another, you are inventing the kind of relationship that's deeply satisfying to both of you.

People are addicted to lying to preserve the illusion. If we as a nation didn't love to be lied to, politicians would tell us the truth.

BONNIE EAKER WEIL, PHD:

By keeping this secret, the chance that you'll repeat this pattern and cheat again is much higher than if you fess up. The chance for changing the marriage, and for fixing this wake-up "cry for help," is nonexistent if you keep the secret. But my caveat is that you don't want to tell if it's only about getting it off your chest in an effort to feel better. You need to choose the right time. Is your spouse going through something traumatic? For example, is her mother hospitalized? Is one of your kids battling an illness? Is there a history of adultery in your wife's family, in which case this will be particularly difficult for her to hear? The point is, don't bombard her with something she can't handle at this time.

If you decide not to tell your wife right now—she's too vulnerable or a grudge holder—then find out why you did this. There's an emptiness inside you need to address. Don't tell yourself, "Oh, a one-night stand is no big deal." It's always a big deal. It's a disease for which I developed a theory, called "the biochemical craving for connection" and thrill-seeking. You're self-medicating rather than looking at what's going on. The affair needs to be addressed, not minimized.

" MY TAKE "

Both sets of experts subscribe to the philosophy that adultery is the forgivable sin. Confession is good for the soul and ultimately for the marriage.

Dr. Gay Hendricks and Dr. Kathlyn Hendricks cut through the litany of excuses a "guilty" partner makes to justify keeping the volatile secret by stating the über-truth: Withholding of information is typically due to not wanting to face the pain and wrath of the betrayed. However, I must add a qualifier to the experts' contention that the act of confession matters more than the act to which one is confessing. On a personal level, I would find it easier to hear from my husband that he'd hesitated for weeks to tell me his job was on the chopping block rather than the secret he'd been hiding was infidelity. The former lie, while upsetting, would seem to be more about his personality than with his issues with me and/or with us as a couple.

But secrets do eat away at an intimate connection. And the giving up of confidences can provide an opening. As Dr. Weil points out, timing is important and if it seems better for the "innocent" spouse to delay the unburdening, the one who was unfaithful should begin the process of self-discovery. And while a one-night stand may seem more a misstep than an ongoing affair, know it is one that could have been sidestepped.

It's important to address the steps between confession and its role in the creation of a brave, new intimacy. The immediate aftermath will be brutally raw and totally heartbreaking. There is much to be aired, discussed, explained—it is not a quick process.

The person who has committed the infidelity must be prepared to be as patient as possible with his or her partner's lack of trust, lava-hot anger, and deep-seated pain. If the betrayee ultimately wants to repair the marriage, he or she is much better served after the initial shock subsides to be self-reflective rather than self-righteous. Ultimately, punishment is not the aim. The goal is accountability and repair. Both parties should seek outside support from friends and/or therapists to help them deal with the complicated web of their feelings.

To be human is to be flawed. Two flawed humans coming together to create a life do not automatically become perfect beings. They will make mistakes. A one-night stand is a big one but it doesn't mean the perpetrator of this marital "felony" is evil—just floundering. Forgivable sin, remember?

It is what the cheater does postmistake that counts. Everyone deserves a second chance. A third? Well, that might be more problematic.

My husband cheated on me. The affair is over and he's apologized plenty, but I know he feels that my coldness drove him to it. Could that be true?

JOHN GRAY, PhD:

While it doesn't excuse his behavior, quite often what drives a man to cheat is his wife's indifference, lack of appreciation, and lack of responsiveness sexually. Personally, if I have a great weekend with my wife I don't look at other women except as works of art.

However, first he has to understand that his betrayal, his offense, landed him in "jail" and his partner will decide how long he's "locked up." This means that for anywhere from three to nine months, which is the length of time it takes to heal a wound, the wife needs to be able to bring up the affair. She doesn't want to be insulting in the process. But when he does something upsetting, it's okay to say, "I don't trust your going to hang out with your friend Roger. Last time you lied to me and cheated."

During this period he has to understand she won't be as loving as he'd like. There will be progress and relapses. And it may take a while for her to be ready for sex. She has to understand that if her anger and hurt persist, it's not all stemming from the affair. Her husband's betrayal is triggering hurt from the past. For instance, it can be a breath of fresh air for her to look at unresolved pain from her relationship with her father growing up. What will destroy the marriage is if the husband keeps having affairs or if the wife can't ultimately forgive him or let go of the rage. But once he has served his "time," his record should be clean. She needs to appreciate that he's changing and stop punishing him.

It's typically easier for a man to let go of an affair because for him there's not an emotional attachment. Now that he sees how much his wife was hurt, he can change his behavior. He can help repair her trust by meeting her needs, but she has to do her part too. It shouldn't be a free ride because she's the "victim." The past can't be changed. The most important thing here is that the wound gets healed.

During the recovery period the wife can ask for things she wants from the husband. Perhaps she can ask for romantic dates, for him to make time to explore feelings, to talk about things that occurred during the week. The point is to ask for what she needs in the present, not get caught up in the past.

MICHAEL D. ZENTMAN, PHD:

No, she didn't drive him to cheat. Yes, her coldness was a factor. If he couldn't tolerate her coldness, though, he had other choices. Instead of having an affair he could have said, "I can't stand this. What can I do to warm you up? Should we try counseling?" What her behavior did was make the relationship vulnerable to such a breach.

However, people who have an affair often have a hard time taking full responsibility and apologizing. For instance, President Clinton initially denied his philandering. But once the evidence is unequivocally laid out, the perpetrator usually confesses.

He has to promise to stop all contact with his affair partner. It's understandable he won't want to talk about all the little details, but his wife may have lots of questions: "I thought you were playing golf and you were seeing her?" The wife was living a whole other reality and feels she has to correct the erroneous information. It's like when you view a car accident. You don't want to look but inevitably you do: "Was she better than me? Tell me the gory details."

The most important thing is, does the person who cheated really want to allow his partner to re-establish trust? If so, he has to be completely transparent with his wife. If she wants to call and check up that he's really on the golf course, that's her right. Often the person who had the affair gets angry; he feels he's told her he's trustworthy now and that should be enough. It's not.

That's not to say a marriage can't survive an affair. It can be an opportunity. The couple can return to the way things were before or go to a level of greater intimacy. That probably won't happen without therapy. Newlyweds typically are in a honeymoon phase—they're getting everything from their spouse they got or wanted from their parents. Suddenly it shifts and they experience some aspect of the deprivation they experienced with their parents. The spouse goes from being the provider of the solution to being the problem. That's the wedge driving people apart.

For instance, if the wife has always been cold, why did the husband choose her? Perhaps he had a parent who was suffocating, so he chose someone who was the polar opposite, only now that's become a problem. It's about both partners becoming self-focused enough to see their contributions to the problem: How dare you turn out to be who you are versus who I wanted you to be? Gaining insight won't make her become a whole other, much warmer person, but chances are there's enough water in the well to keep him hydrated.

" MY TAKE "

I love Dr. Gray's jail sentence analogy. No disputing that an unfaithful husband deserves a harsh prison term for the grievous crime directed at his wife's heart. However, if there is no hope of eventual parole, what incentive is there for him to work at repairing her trust? Still, the three-to-nine-month time frame might be optimistic. The pain of betrayal is a long-lingering one. The husband does want to be tossed a life raft—the knowledge that however long it takes, she is working to put the affair behind them.

The wife, for her part, as Dr. Gray points out, should realize that if her anger is boundless, it's likely the infidelity is dredging up feelings from an earlier hurt. She needs to stay in the present. The more she can detach from the emotional quicksand that occurs from becoming obsessed with events in the past, the more she will own her life rather than being held hostage by a vat of pain. It's a real energy zapper!

Both experts believe the wife's coldness was a precipitating factor in her partner's straying. But as Dr. Zentman underscores, this doesn't get the husband off the hook. He made the choice to cheat. And if the marriage has any hope of resurrection, the husband must immediately cut all ties to his ex-paramour. The therapist also makes a strong case that it is crucial to grasp that the initial attraction to the spouse—he or she was the antithesis of a difficult parent—is what can cause the breach. Once a couple stop being imprisoned by the unconscious wish for their partner to fulfill childhood needs, they can begin to forge an adult connection.

A little more about the F word: forgiveness. It's never easy to absolve a cheating spouse, even one who "apologizes plenty." There may be a fear that if the betrayed partner eventually says to the spouse, "Okay, fresh slate," it will be taken as a license to cheat again: "Hey I got away with it once." Or the feeling might be that no amount of suffering is too great for the reformed cheater. He or she or will never understand the pain that comes from discovering that the gift of trust bestowed on a marriage partner was misplaced. Let the punishment continue.

Let me play devil's advocate. Forgiveness is a sine qua non of relationships—once a person can truly pardon another for messing up, she can forgive herself. That's the most important task that needs to happen, and the hardest one to accomplish. Often the rage a person has for her partner is partly projection of "offenses" for which she hates herself: "If I hadn't been so cold he wouldn't have strayed." Leaving the anger behind paves the way for creating a marriage that is inviolable.

I've never physically cheated on my wife, but I've grown very close to a coworker. Is there such a thing as emotional infidelity?

MONA R. BARBERA, PhD:

Yes, and it can be as damaging, or even more damaging, than a purely sexual affair. Emotional infidelity occurs when the partner gets his or her emotional needs met by an outsider. This usually happens because those needs are not being met in the marriage. If someone feels those little twinges starting to occur when they're with a colleague or friend it's important to look at the marriage and ask, "What is missing?" Also ask, "Why am I not asking for this in my marriage? Am I afraid of my partner's anger or depression or that we won't make it?"

Having these conversations with your spouse is not easy. Things can be said that are very triggering and scary to one's sense of security and self-worth. To backtrack, our initial choice of partner is typically based on one of three things—feeling a sense of security around this person, or a sense of excitement, or sharing a tremendous sense of emotional intimacy, that connection we've always yearned for. The reality is that we need all these things with a partner. If there is just one, a few years down the road we might be saying, "Why did I choose someone who makes me feel safe but with whom there's absolutely no excitement?" Or "Why did I choose someone who's so emotionally satisfying but he can't hold a job?"

You need to look inside yourself and see why you chose a partner in such a skewed way. This is about you, not something to blame your partner for. If you can't get all three qualities with someone, you might wind up separating. But if you're really honest with yourself and your partner—if you can have those difficult conversations about what is lacking, and if it's possible to find it—the two of you might find a flow together.

How can you tell if things might work out? Perhaps in the past you weren't ready to be vulnerable in some of these areas, but now you are. Again, be honest about what you are really experiencing, the things you judge yourself harshly for feeling. You might find a solution you never anticipated. The key is to reveal stuff that isn't comfortable. Once you start the ball rolling your partner can do it too, and soon there might not be a desire to go outside the marriage for connection.

Sue Johnson, EdD:

Yes, emotional infidelity does exist, but people don't understand the ramifications because they don't understand the nature of love. Attachment theory says the deepest need of all humans is to have someone who will come when they call, to whom they matter, to whom they're precious. When that need is not met in a primary relationship, everything starts to go wrong. People start confiding in an outsider. This is how emotional infidelity evolves. It seems innocent, but in their bones they sense that if they turn elsewhere to share deep feelings and longings instead of turning to their marriage partner, it's setting up a competing attachment.

This doesn't mean one can't have very good friends, but love is a special kind of emotional bond that is wired in by millions of years of evolution. People have this incredible need to regard their relationship as a safe haven. It's our basic survival system. However, they don't understand that longing; it even causes shame. Yet according to new research, when people can't experience this bond with their partner their brain goes into primal panic. The loneliness of trying to connect is not just an unpleasant sensation, but is encoded into the brain in the same place as physical pain. Science tells us that people can have all kinds of disagreements and fights, but if they can be emotionally close to their partner they'll be okay.

When a couple get stuck in really negative patterns with one another—being demanding, withdrawing, and so on—what often results is that their behavior pushes away their partner. The incredible loneliness one then feels creates a natural tendency to turn to someone else to be validated and emotionally connected. But the more they confide in someone else, the less they risk with their spouse, and that's a threat to the primary relationship. This other person is now seen as safe and their partner as dangerous. It's a sign. Heed it.

" MY TAKE "

By wending down different but equally fascinating byways, the therapists arrive at the same conclusion: Emotional infidelity can cause disease in a healthy marriage, and thus should come with a warning label like the ones on cigarette packs. Dr. Barbera speaks of how people choose a spouse based on a subconscious search for someone who can fulfill a deep, unmet need. Unfortunately, in the process, two other equally important inner needs are often ignored; needs that, once they inevitably begin making their presence felt, will signal the end of the honeymoon period and the beginning of dissatisfaction with the partner. The question then becomes: Do couples deal with those "twinges" of discontent by forging a new, more honest bond with one another, or go elsewhere for that connection fix?

Dr. Johnson discusses the need to connect with the hardwiring of the brain, which makes people instinctually seek safe haven with a love object. In primitive times, having someone dependable in one's corner could literally mean the difference between life and death. Now it just feels that way.

Both experts state that while emotional infidelity springs from deep in that childhood place, it can have very dangerous adult consequences for the marriage.

Here are signs that one is uncomfortably perched on that slippery slope between an "innocent" friendship with a member of the opposite sex and viewing that friend the way the spouse was once regarded—as alluring and indispensable. You are:

- Exchanging e-mails with this friend in an account you've password-protected so the spouse doesn't stumble across them
- Having delicious, long meals with said friend that are kept secret from the spouse
- Sharing gossip and stories with this person instead of with the spouse
- Starting to feel like the friend understands you better than anyone does

Did reading this list lead to a hot-under-the collar feeling? The platonic friend is a Band-Aid, not a cure to the original deep wounding that occurred in childhood. The way to resolve these wounds is to work through the core issues that have been such a factor in the marital relationship, not start from scratch with someone new.

How can I tell if my spouse is having a cyber-affair?

STEPHEN W. SIMPSON, PHD:

What is the state of your marriage? Why are you suspicious? The researcher Dr. David Schnarch talks about differentiation and how important it is for a couple to be able to define themselves as separate from their partner. When two marital partners feel good about themselves, have their own interests, and can disagree about issues without becoming anxious, they are at much less risk of an extramarital affair.

The computer has made cheating a lot easier. A lot of people who wouldn't have had affairs before this technology now will, because they can log on anywhere. Some people feel justified in their actions because they're not taking it to a physical level. But if you're being romantic, emotionally intimate with anyone other than your spouse, it's cheating. The marital attachment is being threatened.

Here are some probable signs something is going on: Does it feel like your spouse is pulling away, wanting to spend a lot of time on the computer? Does he stay up late after you've gone to bed to go online? Does he wait to go online until you are asleep?

The practical way to find out for sure is to dig into his or her computer. But you should ask your spouse. Don't go on the attack. That will make him defensive versus wanting to reassure you. Be vulnerable. Say, "I feel like you're pulling away from me and I'm scared. It seems like you spend a lot of time on the computer talking to other people."

With all that people do online these days, it's possible he's spending hours checking out the Fantasy Baseball League. In that case, your suspicions say more about you than about him.

LESLIEBETH WISH, EDD:

If a person wants to hide something from you, he or she can. But there are warning signs of a cyber-dalliance.

Is your spouse staying up late at night alone? Have there been any major changes in his routine? For example, some women report their husband suddenly becoming more affectionate. Or wanting to try new things sexually, things that make them uncomfortable. Cybersex is a stimulant. Other women, however, report their husband's suddenly acting less affectionate. The key is that there is something different going on. Other potential signs of a cyber and/or real-world affair: There is suddenly not enough money to pay bills. It could be the husband is buying sex on the Internet. Or he says he is having all-day meetings and/or working weekends.

What should you do if it seems your spouse is cheating? Ask yourself, "How am I part of the problem? Have I been acting differently? Have I been distant, acting angry, not making the marriage a priority?"

The question of whether or not you should confront this with your mate head-on depends on what type of marriage you have. Some relationships are strong enough that you can ask, "What's going on, honey? Things haven't been right for a long time," and get a real answer. Other times you have to opt for action versus talking. For example, if you've been an avoider, change your behavior to be more engaged in the relationship. Say, "Honey, let's go hiking. I've wanted us to do that for a while." You have to know your partner to decide which approach to take.

" MY TAKE "

To confront or not to confront a spouse about those niggling suspicions? That is the question within this question, and it nets conflicting answers from the experts. Dr. Simpson advocates (along with possibly breaking into the mate's computer) bringing up the issue in a nonaccusatory, emotionally vulnerable style. I agree this is a topic that must be broached in a manner that will elicit honesty—and hopefully, affection.

There is merit in Dr. Wish's suggestion to gauge a partner's receptivity before popping the question (in other words, if his default attitude is commonly aloofness and/or hostility, it's possible the response will be more bluster than truth). However, not remarking in some fashion on the elephant in the room, instead dancing around the burgeoning estrangement by acting differently, might be too passive and back door-ish, not to mention extremely stressful to engineer. It's not essential to voice the suspicion, but open the door to some sort of discussion. Express willingness to do whatever it takes to become closer, which speaks to Dr. Wish's point about engaging in self-analysis: What role have I played? Part of a discussion would be asking what your partner feels the problems are in the marriage, and his or her thoughts about potential solutions.

Last, don't discount Dr. Simpson's provocative closer. If the spouse is 100 percent worthy of trust, yada yada, why does the suspicious partner go to these dark, angry places? Is it a pattern of needing to feel that a loved one will inevitably prove to be a betrayer?

More signs of potential cyber-cheating: Is there a refusal to answer questions about what he or she is doing while online? Does he or she shut down the computer as soon as someone walks into the room?

The website *www.chatcheaters.com* debates the pros and cons of cyber-snooping on a mate. It is possible to do more than just check the computer's history to find out whether he or she has been visiting chat rooms and personals sites. Chatcheaters.com offers resources to aid in purchasing computer-monitoring software that tracks every movement. However, after going this route it's harder to subsequently get away with thinking, "Oh, I'm not a scheming person. It's not my fault I accidentally meandered around his Apple and found a worm."

After confronting him or her, be prepared to hear that online flirting isn't really cheating. The rebuttal can be, "Then why was it something you needed to keep hidden from me?"

FIELD REPORT

Three years into our marriage, when we were going through a rough patch, my husband confessed he'd had a one-night stand. Understandably, I freaked out, calling him every name in the book and demanding he leave the house. He cried and swore that he loved me and all he wanted to do was make things right. What did I need? Could we go to a therapist? My pride and hurt demanded I kick him to the curb; he was a thoroughly malignant excuse for a human being. But my love and wonderful friends eventually convinced me to look inward. I realized my husband hadn't mangled things alone. I'd helped. We went to the therapist, did a lot of work, and today are happier than ever.

~ *Name Withheld, 39, New York City*

IF I HAD A DO-OVER

❦

Barry Cohen
Lake Hopatcong, New Jersey

"It's better to forgive than to blame."

In 1991 my marriage of seven years fell apart. It happened after I started my own business. My fatal flaw is being a workaholic. My wife and I didn't spend enough quality time together. She became involved with someone else and after our divorce, they married.

I was very bitter. For the first few years I spent all my time working to pay the bills. I also read a lot of self-help books that gave the message that it takes two and no matter how wrong one person was. During the marriage I'd been thinking, "Why doesn't she understand I'm working so hard for us?"

I started dating, but there was nothing serious. I never stopped loving my wife. Since there were no children we'd had no contact after the breakup. Seven years after the divorce, she called. Her father, to whom I'd once been close, had died. As it turned out, her marriage was on the verge of breaking up.

We started seeing each other. I was cautious, not wanting to leap. After a couple of months she moved back in. We remarried. That was eleven years ago.

I jokingly say to people, "I like my second wife better than the first one!" We had to do a certain amount of growing up. We consider each other's feelings more now.

A close friend once quoted, "The opposite of love isn't hate. It's indifference." I was never indifferent to my wife. If it is real love, you need to be able to see past the hurt and anger, acknowledge your part and to forgive.

CHAPTER EIGHT

HANDLING THE ROUGH PATCHES

For couples facing a crisis, the danger is twofold. First there is the trauma, be it the illness or death of a loved one, loss of a job, infertility, or other sad challenge. Then there is the chaos often resulting in the relationship, especially when each person handles trauma differently. It is essential to learn both the tools that can bring you closer as well as strategies for avoiding the traps that can tear you apart. In this chapter, marriage experts who specialize in crisis counseling provide dead-on advice on how to handle a host of potential minefields.

My husband's been unemployed for five months. My salary is floating us, but his self-esteem is taking a huge hit. He used to be this macho man but now he's more and more insecure. How can I convince him he's still worthy of my respect?

KAREN SHERMAN, PhD:

The wife can't convince her husband to have self-worth, but she can let him know she thinks he's worthy. First, it's crucial not to invalidate his emotions. She needs to say something like, "I understand you feel terrible. Men identify themselves in our society by the fact that they're breadwinners." Then she can add a more personal statement: "But our relationship is based far more on who we are as people. I am supportive of you. I am here for you. We will get through this."

What he does after this is up to him. A wife tends to analyze and want to talk. A man is typically reluctant to have long conversations. He'd rather say simply, "I feel really lousy. I don't have a job," and leave it there. He's voiced his feelings. A woman trying to make her husband feel better might have the opposite effect. She can ask his help on things that can build his feeling of competence and then show him she appreciates his efforts. But don't go overboard. He's not stupid. He can sense when his wife is trying to feed his ego.

PAUL DUNION, EdD, LPC:

This is all about the female's need to influence her husband. She shouldn't try to convince him he's deserving of her respect; that's beyond her control. But many women in this situation would try to change the husband's mindset, and wind up feeling stupid or inadequate for not pulling it off. She can be his ally, but building self-esteem is an internal process.

It's a big deal for couples to learn what is under their control and what is not. Most are not clear about the distinction. But in this case she's infantilizing him. This is a dynamic she needs to escape from, as much for her sake as for his. This question is a great metaphor for getting clear about limits and not attempting the impossible in the name of love.

" MY TAKE "

Remember the famous Eleanor Roosevelt quote, "No one can make you feel inferior without your consent"? According to Dr. Sherman and Dr. Dunion, the other side of the coin is true as well. You can't will another person to buck up and get some self-esteem or else!

Both experts offer sexist-sounding but basically on-target interpretations of this particular dilemma, which can bedevil a couple when one of life's inevitable setbacks materializes. When the blow affects her mate, a woman's instinct is typically to analyze and comfort. A man whose competence has been called into question, however, tends to want to crawl into his lair and lick his wounds.

Dr. Sherman's suggestion that a woman subtly push her husband toward performing tasks at which he excels to feed his ego is a good one. Dr. Dunion points out that it is essential for spouses to realize what is in their power to "fix" and what is not—most things fall in the latter category, alas! The ability to let go, to not be fixated on the need to create a particular result, is a skill that will benefit not just the marriage but each person as an individual.

It would be helpful for the wife to look at what lies beneath her compulsion to raise her husband's self-esteem. Why is it so important for her to induce him to feel better? Obviously no one wants to see a loved one in pain, but it seems likely that more than empathy is involved in this case.

Is she worried that if her husband begins questioning how he feels about himself, he'll question his regard for her as well? Does she have a fear that if he is incapable of taking care of himself he'll be incapable of taking care of her?

We choose partners who trigger us to act out dysfunctional childhood relationship dynamics, dynamics we subconsciously wish to change. For instance, perhaps her husband's former macho persona was similar to that of her father, who was tyrannical and made her feel inept? That's an awful feeling but one that is familiar, and thus safe.

We typically run from emotions that cause distress, but if the wife can deal with the discomfort raised by her husband's new insecurities, she can be a detective and begin examining her own patterns and why she is trapped in them. Only then can she be on the road to change. Freeing herself from the places where she is stuck can help liberate her husband as well.

My wife's alcoholism is out of control. She doesn't think she has a problem. How can I get her to seek help?

KEITH ABLOW, MD:

The partner of someone struggling with an addiction needs to tell the truth. Gather the courage to tell your spouse what you've observed with empathy and clarity. Offer support but be honest about what you've seen and how it makes you feel. If your wife's focus on drinking renders her emotionally unavailable to you, share that.

Another important step is to admit you're deeply affected by your wife's problem. Ask yourself, "Why am I settling for life with an addict? What in my background could have led to my involvement with someone who often makes me feel worthless?" Is this someplace you want to be?

Third, be aware addictions don't die easily. This is a long-term problem for both of you. An addict gravitates to alcohol as a distraction from underlying issues she's not ready to look at. If she stops drinking she'll switch to a secondary addiction—work, shopping, whatever. Understand that living with an addict, even a recovering one, requires much vigilance.

You need clear-cut boundaries. Sometimes an addict will improve, but only when she knows a choice must be made between the alcohol and the person she loves. Sometimes you'll have to say, "Honey, you smell of alcohol. We're not going out tonight. I'm sorry if this troubles you, but I need to be comfortable. When you chose to drink you opened the door to my worrying about it." There will be times during the recovery that you think she's had a drink even when she hasn't; this results from all the trauma the addiction has inflicted on you over time. You can err on the side of being careful by saying, "Honey, I need you to take a breathalyzer test before we go out."

The idea isn't to make your wife feel guilty. You need to respect and understand the hold alcohol has on your partner. The roots of addiction are deep.

Marriage is difficult in the best of circumstances. Adding the complication of addiction makes it that much more challenging. Things will never be perfect, but you need to know there is potential for improvement.

What better love story can there be than someone who stands by a spouse, helps her get to the bottom of her addiction by learning about the vulnerabilities that fueled it? You learn about yourself as well. This is loving someone for much more than her sparkling blue eyes! This is a story to tell your children one day: "This is what we went through. We didn't like it, but we didn't run away and wound up stronger."

GAY HENDRICKS, PHD, AND KATHLYN HENDRICKS, PHD, ADT:

The first thing is to show your vulnerability and describe to your partner the actual impact of the addiction on you. This can help cut through her fog: "I feel very sad and scared that the drinking will take you over and I'll lose you. I don't know what to do. I feel myself getting more and more distant." Then ask if she is willing to resolve the issue.

The literature is clear: She has to make the decision and truly be committed to stop drinking. You don't want to get caught up in a push/pull with your mate—alternately trying to rescue or control her. This simply enables her and prolongs the addiction. Criticizing her over and over will send her back to the bottle.

This is a difficult situation and best handled in the same way you would the aftermath of a betrayal—one person needs to start opening up and creating a space for honest communication.

We've seen this scenario go both ways. If your wife is willing to change, you can support her efforts to get into whatever kind of program can help. If she isn't willing, know that you can go round and round for decades in the rescue, control, relapse cycle.

" MY TAKE "

The message is clear: Addiction takes a heartbreaking toll on both partners in a marriage.

Dr. Ablow makes several excellent points. Even if the wife decides to commit to the treatment, recovery is a slow process. Unless she commits as well to dealing with the underlying issues that she began drinking to avoid facing, she is more likely to switch to another addiction than become sober. Recovery is a long-term journey, a road strewn with many detours and potholes. And what in the enabler's psychological makeup caused him to commit to a relationship that infers such second-class-citizen status? Think of the roller-coaster ride experienced by a "mistress" involved with a married man. He says he loves her, but the pull of his relationship with his wife, no matter how dysfunctional, keeps winning out.

Dr. Gay Hendricks and Dr. Kathlyn Hendricks present the hard-to-swallow truth: One can continue enabling a partner by sticking around, alternately berating and beseeching, while she continues drinking and making empty promises, or accept her decision to drink or quit and proceed from there.

Both experts point out that this addiction is probably the strongest test a marriage will face. If the couple can triumph over this they've acquired the tools and tenacity to stay together forever.

The alcoholic loves her partner but is controlled by her addiction. Her partner must try not to take personally all the times she continues to put her need to drink ahead of her desire to make him happy. She would love to make him happy but that cannot be the motivation for her to quit. She can only quit when she's doing it for herself. And she has to love herself enough to quit; not an easy task, for that means facing her demons.

She'll say she's putting her marriage first, but addicts lie. It's part of the sickness. The husband is not doing the wife a favor by believing her promises to stop drinking, and then becoming shocked and contemptuous when he finds her stash in the sugar jar. She can't help herself—until she decides she can, and asks for support.

A better solution is for him to join Al-Anon, the AA-sponsored program for families of alcoholics. There the spouse can get the support and information he desperately needs in this tumultuous time.

This husband shouldn't stay futilely, hoping the wife will quit. He should leave if he needs to. That is ultimately best for both people.

We lost a child, but instead of bringing us together this mutual tragedy is driving us apart. Can we avoid divorce?

JANE GREER, DSW, LMFT:

It's natural to experience the loss as your own and to expect support and understanding from your partner. He or she is in the same place. This loss has triggered a whole range of emotional upheaval that brought on a childlike, dependent state of mind. You're like kids racing around with cut knees looking for mommy to make it better.

Grief is all-consuming. You are depleted of emotional and physical energy and your capacity to give to another is tapped to the max. Yet a relationship is about giving. As each of you become needier, you ask more of the other—whether for more understanding or favors or support—"I'm too tired and upset to have sex tonight. You should understand."

But the reality is you're both adults and have to take some responsibility for dealing with your own pain. The knee-jerk reaction is anger. When you lose a child it's very hard not to be blaming, and the easiest one to pin blame on is your spouse; maybe not for what happened, but for not being able to stop it. You might also be projecting your own feelings of guilt onto your partner. It's important to look at your feelings of self-blame.

The most important thing is to recognize that you are in the same boat and to acknowledge and empathize with each other's pain and devastation. Realize that he or she loved your child as much as you did.

Understand that this is a transitional time. It is important to become more tolerant of your partner's as well as your own limitations. This allows you to begin to change your expectations of what he or she should be doing for you so that you will be left with fewer feelings of being disappointed.

One of the best ways to cope with loss is to focus on creating a new direction in your marriage. Spend time together processing your grief, perhaps finding ways to keep your child alive in spirit. Commit to keeping your family together in honor of your child even though right now things feel fractured.

When the time is right, try new activities—take a trip, go dancing. This will help you move forward together instead of separately.

Lee H. Baucom, PhD:

This husband and wife base their sense of being a family on their child instead of on being a couple. They are not starting from a place of, "We will get through this together no matter what." Instead of relying on one another as a point of comfort, they are taking their grief out on their partner. They are probably confiding in friends and family rather than in each other.

A therapist would try to get them to lean on each other for support, to start thinking of themselves as a "we." A couple in this situation needs to do grief work; that is, share with one another what the loss means. It's then helpful to do a "Vision Statement": What does their marriage mean to each of them? What do they want it to be about going forward?

Part of this work is figuring out the resistance to being a "we." Does it stem from a fear of intimacy, of abandonment (as they've been "abandoned" by their child), a fear that if they make themselves vulnerable they will be left or lose a sense of self? The couple needs to explore these feelings, to hear one another speak of the pain and struggles each is facing. Very often we hear the anger from our partner and react to that, not realizing the fear underneath the volatility.

Once they're at a more vulnerable place together they can share the burden of the grief and move forward.

" MY TAKE "

Dr. Greer stresses the primal nature of this most devastating of losses. The death of a child can cause a time warp, ripping away the veneer of maturation and turning us back into children. A person in a pure "id" place is me, me, me. It is too frightening to gaze inward into the yawning void of loss; easier to attempt to "fill" oneself with junk—the temporary sugar high of displacing pain and self-blame onto someone else.

Dr. Baucom's advice focuses less specifically on the impact of the death of a child and hammers home the point that if a couple's algebra is $1 + 1 = 1$, a trauma of this magnitude can rupture their tenuous sense of couple-dom.

What was the state of the marriage before this tragedy? If there was already some degree of estrangement, it can be especially hard to return to that "we" place.

Something that might help the couple toward this goal is to honor not their similarities but their differences. People grieve at a different pace and in a different way. One partner might be more prone to throw himself or herself into outside activities to distract from the pain, while the other is aghast at the thought of making any effort to resume a state of normalcy. "Different" doesn't mean "lesser than." Both spouses feel the loss equally, even if one's way of showing it may initially seem strange to the other.

There is a societal expectation that men and women deal differently with emotion, that the husband should have a stiff upper lip while the wife is expected to be a walking manufacturer of tears. Try not to unconsciously carry around this prejudice if a spouse's behavior seems atypical to his or her sex. Two people suffered a loss and are entitled to grieve in any way that feels natural.

Make connections with other couples in similar circumstances. Grief is grief no matter how it is expressed, and better shared. A helpful resource is Compassionate Friends (*www.compassionatefriends.org*), a support group for families who have lost a child.

Depression runs in my family. When I occasionally go into a deep funk my husband just tells me to snap out of it and I retreat even further. Can we break this pattern?

SHEILA BENDER, PHD:

The couple is looking at this problem from two different vantage points. He's coming at it from the perspective of, "why can't she just snap out of it?" She is countering that depression is part of who she is. She's probably had it throughout her life.

She needs to understand that there are ways to come out of it, but he needs to understand she can't instantaneously snap-to. He's giving a simple solution and she's unable to accept that solution.

To gain perspective on why it's not a snap for her, I would ask him to find something that's not easy for him. Say he's carrying extra weight or has a tyrannical boss, problems he finds very difficult to "fix." Handling depression for her is like losing twenty pounds for him. Once there's an opening, there's some common territory and they will be less irritated with each other.

She needs to see that people can overcome impossible-seeming obstacles. It's helpful to look at areas where she has made concrete changes in the past. If she's a spiritual person, she can look toward faith to help her.

Advances are being made in the treatment of depression all the time. They should do some research into new treatments. There's a wonderful book about cellular chemistry—*The Biology of Belief*, by Bruce Lipton, PhD, which is a brilliant look at science and the spirit.

Another helpful approach is to use genograms. This is a pictorial map commonly used by family therapists. It's like an elaborate family tree centering on the emotional experiences each partner lived through in his or her family and how these experiences affect their romantic relationships now. Did her parents have depression? What treatments did they try, and how effective were they? Perhaps if one parent was a drinker and/or there was a lot of fighting in her home and she never saw a good solution to these problems she grew up feeling, "I am doomed." Just looking at this reactive belief system she's held can help her begin to search for proactive approaches.

The main thing the couple should do is view finding something to ease her depression as a joint effort. They want to find solutions, and by doing so they are modeling solution-oriented behavior for their children.

LINDA OLSON, PsyD:

Without a doubt they can break this pattern. When he puts her down for being depressed, she feels devalued and dismissed. She responds by disconnecting from her partner. Unfortunately a healthy relationship is all about a couple feeling connected. Skills the husband should learn to aid communication are to mirror, validate, and empathize. When you get into trouble in a relationship, using these principles can repair the connection. They revolve around becoming intentional.

For example, he says, "Sweetie, tell me more about the depression." She responds, "I start to feel depressed when such and such happens." He listens and mirrors: "Oh, you feel depressed when I blow you off and say you shouldn't feel depressed." She agrees. He validates: "It makes sense that you would feel that way when I do that." He shows empathy by saying, "I imagine if I show you I understand how you feel, that can help you feel better." The language he uses doesn't matter. We've all experienced depression at some time or other, so he can imagine what it feels like. What counts is that he shows her he has the ability to put himself in her shoes.

He probably hates to see her in pain, so wants to dismiss it by telling her curtly to feel better. That doesn't repair the rupture; it causes further damage. He needs to get over himself and how he feels and get into how his partner feels. What she needs is for him to just be with her emotionally, to connect.

" MY TAKE "

Both experts offer heartening takes on this dilemma. Any couple caught up in this dynamic should pay heed to Dr. Bender's assessment that they are operating on diametrically opposed tracks—and that each track is a journey to nowhere. Being told to snap out of it made for a memorable line in *Moonstruck* but it's a terrible communication strategy, guaranteed to anger, depress, and cause a partner to mentally disengage.

I love Dr. Bender's suggestion that the snap-happy spouse learn to empathize with his wife's position by imagining a situation that he finds depressing and complex. It is equally vital that the wife look at her belief that depression is hard-wired into her psyche, thus something over which she has no control. And last, if the couple can come to view the wife's battle over controlling the depression as their project versus hers alone, it becomes something that brings them together rather than a divisive element.

Dr. Olson's insight that the husband curtly dismisses his wife's depression because it's difficult for him to deal with her pain is a powerful one, and her instruction on how he can learn to connect with his wife through the mirror, validate, empathize principle is sound. However, advice is still needed on how to make the horse—errr, husband—want to drink the water. How to make that happen is where my input comes in.

It's important that the depressed person look at the spouse's point of view and not feel that he or she is the only one in pain, and thus the only one in need of succor.

A relationship between two people is a constant balancing act. One partner's happy mood can be infectious. But as sympathetic as someone may be to a spouse's habitual depression, it's difficult to be around constant sadness. The emotionally stable spouse likely wants to offer a listening ear and/or warm hug but it's hard for him to do so, having likely been rebuffed on many occasions. The "bystander" to this chronic emotional pain might feel helpless and/or angry that his presence seems to make no difference. Yet he squashes those emotions, not wanting to further upset the spouse who is the Designated Depressed Person in the marriage. While it's noble to try not to further burden the partner, those feelings have to go somewhere or they will eventually emerge in the form of anger or passive aggressiveness—snap out of it!

Both partners need to realize that the non- or at least less-miserable person in the marriage needs a place to vent those emotions. A punching bag, great friend, and/or therapist are some options that come to mind. And when the depressed partner stabilizes, it's good to initiate a conversation about what it feels like to watch a loved one be sad. Sharing emotions is healthy; keeping things inside leads to mutual disconnect.

Depression can create emotional paralysis. As the nonparalyzed part of the marital team, don't encourage the partner to keep a stiff upper lip, snap out of it, or ride it out. Encourage her to seek help.

I just stumbled upon a bank account my husband kept secret for many months. He says it's not a big deal, but I feel so betrayed. What should I do?

Dr. Bonnie Eaker Weil, PhD:

There's no such thing as an innocent financial fib. You have a right to feel betrayed. What he did is a subtle form of cheating, a hostile act. Not so much about the lying or omitting, but about the deceit that destroys intimacy, trust, or passion.

Typically there is a lot of shame, blame, fear, and feelings of abandonment around money. No wonder then that it's a breeding ground for power struggles. Your spouse blows $2,000 on a new computer so you spend two days at a spa—tit for tat, like bickering siblings.

Many couples are fight-phobic, outwardly doing their best to avoid conflict. However, pushing things under the rug in an attempt to have a "polite" marriage leads to acting-out behaviors such as adultery and financial infidelity.

The bank account is a symptom of the threat that can destroy a marriage—deceit. Look at your role in what's happened and then confront your mate in an empathetic, nonjudgmental, non-blaming way. Say something like, "I know I've been working long hours and am hardly ever home. I can understand that you're really pissed at me or maybe worried that since I haven't been available I'm going to leave. Hiding the money is your way of telling me you're not happy. I'm willing to do whatever it takes to bring this relationship back to where it should be, but I need honesty from you."

By creating safety in this nonjudgmental approach through dialogue there is more chance for your partner to take responsibility and make changes in his behavior. And more chance you can walk in his shoes and understand changes he needs you to make.

In this way you're making yourself vulnerable and holding yourself partially responsible as well. By being empathetic you're helping your husband feel safe enough to be vulnerable and to admit his mistakes as well. It's a good place to begin.

Tania Paredes, LCSW, DCSW:

The wife might be worrying, "If he's keeping the bank account from me, what else is he hiding?" It's an issue of trust. She's probably going to start analyzing every little thing: "Does he really have a late meeting? What is he really doing tonight?"

In order for a relationship to thrive, both partners have to work together. In this case, one partner has betrayed the team. I see a lot of couples that don't subscribe to this philosophy. Their marriage is just a piece of who they are; it doesn't seem in their best interests to share everything going on. While it's fine to focus on yourselves as individuals, there's a fine line between focusing too much on private interests and violating the marriage. You want to keep developing as a person, but keep your partner in the loop.

Maybe the husband just wanted the money to make fun purchases without asking for permission. But doing it behind her back speaks to a communications breakdown, which has resulted in a breakdown of trust. Repair work is in order. He has to look at what factors led him to the point where he kept this large secret, and she has to get to the point where she can work it through: "It's the only time in the span of six years he's hidden something from me. I want to put it to the side and not let this poison the marriage."

He wanted this to come out into the open. Bank accounts are easily discovered!

" MY TAKE "

Both Dr. Eaker Weil and Paredes are on the money—his lie equaled a betrayal. And the wife has a right to the cascade of emotions she is experiencing.

But as Dr. Eaker Weil points out, his lie is a symptom. And while it might provide a jolt of venomous satisfaction to read him the riot act of all riot acts, ultimately the most effective strategy is to use this infidelity as an opportunity to get to the source of the sickness undermining the marriage by doing some self-examination and then approaching the mate in a way that helps him feel safe enough to respond with honesty and without defensiveness.

Paredes's statement that he wanted the lie to be discovered is proof that deep down he wanted the wife to know the depth of his pain, of what he felt driven to do. It was also a cry for help: "Let's save the marriage!"

If I had a nickel for every money lie told in a marriage, I'd have Buffett- and Gates-style wealth. According to a 2005 survey conducted for *Money* magazine, 44 percent of couples consider it acceptable to keep money secrets from one another, at least under certain circumstances. The reason for the subterfuge is not avarice, but a desire to avoid being judged, lectured, found wanting . . . and to avoid a fight. Remember Dr. Eaker Weil's comment about the "polite" marriage.

Men and women typically "lie" about money in different ways. Husbands hide income (hold a secret stash) while wives (think *I Love Lucy*) more often fib about the price of their purchases.

Whether newlyweds or a longtime couple, it is essential to work toward full disclosure. Discuss spending styles. Is one partner's cautiousness rooted in childhood insecurity about where the next meal was coming from, while the other's elaborate gift-giving is his or her way to buy love? Understanding one another's financial personalities will go a long way toward allowing a couple to make peace on this issue.

It's also crucial to develop a financial plan. Stake out goals regarding investments, the children's education, and so on. Don't forget to discuss whether the two of you should pool your money or maintain some individual credit cards and accounts. With everything out in the open, there is no need for a secret stash!

I've been married ten years and have three children. My dirty little secret: My husband is well-meaning, but a few times a year he takes a swing at me, often in front of the kids. He's always sorry. It doesn't

happen a lot and he's never left a bruise, but it's a tough way to live. Short of leaving him, do you have any suggestions?

RENÉE A. COHEN, PhD:

She answers her own question: It's a tough way to live. Actually it's no way to live. Indeed, in many states it is considered child abuse when children are exposed to domestic violence.

The abuser is using power and control. Using these tools intermittently as this husband is doing enforces fear. It is Pavlovian; the wife cannot predict when the violence is going to happen. It's hard to extinguish fear when you never know when the abuse will reoccur. Thus the 90 percent of the time when she is not being hit, the woman is nonetheless being controlled by fear.

She has to ask herself, "Why am I staying?" Is she financially dependent on him? Has he threatened to hurt her if she leaves? Has she told anyone this is happening? It is important for her to understand that there are dynamics from her childhood that make it seem okay to stay in a relationship where not only is she abused, but her children see it is okay to hurt a woman.

The fact that she avoids, denies, rationalizes—"My husband is well-meaning, he's always sorry, he's never left a bruise"—is an attempt to make it go away. Then reality breaks through: It's a tough way to live.

It is her responsibility to protect herself and her children. That is her job. Treatment might be a good idea to help her figure this out, to get help and be educated on parenting skills. If she is not willing to protect herself, she needs to protect her children.

In addition to talking to a therapist, she should share with friends and family what is going on. They can provide empathy and compassion. Keeping the secret helps her not address the abuse with her husband. She needs to say to him, "This can't happen again."

Many abusers were once abused themselves. The husband is teaching his children to go down that road as well. He needs to acknowledge his abuse. Hopefully this couple can go into therapy. And he should do anger management with small groups consisting of other batterers. If this doesn't happen, and he gets violent again, she needs to start reporting it. The courts can't do anything if there is no paperwork.

Then the wife needs to look at a safety plan. Does she have work skills? What time span can she work? What afterschool child care is available? If she gets divorced, will there be some support she'll receive in addition to what she earns? She needs legal as well as emotional support.

The bottom line is that the current situation is unacceptable. Just as the wife needs to learn what unresolved childhood traumas brought her into this relationship, the husband needs to learn the feelings beneath the anger that from time to time give expression in a physically abusive way. The offender must be held accountable and learn skills so he can control himself.

CLOÉ MADANES, PhD, FAPA:

The only behavior you can change is your own. Until recently it was politically incorrect to say that women who get hit are partially responsible for the abuse. However, that is exactly what new research on family violence is pointing to. The wife often starts the cycle of verbal or physical abuse but she's the one who has bruises, sometimes winding up in the hospital, so she is considered the sole victim.

This woman needs to look in an honest way at what she does before he hits her. The husband doesn't hit her out of the blue— has she done something cruel, perhaps insulted him in front of the children?

Even if she is being provocative, of course nothing justifies violence. Research also shows that the biggest victims in cases of domestic violence are the children who see the abuse happen. It's a special kind of terror and despair to watch your mother being hit.

An intervention of sorts is recommended. Both partners need to change their behavior. Look at it this way—a family is a business and this couple should have an executive meeting once a week to discuss serious issues. During the week each should keep a diary of what they're going to discuss and not bring up anything outside the meeting unless there's an emergency. It's better to discuss the violent dynamic in a neutral place, a public place, say the local Chinese restaurant where they have to sit for an hour and not shout.

At the meeting they can discuss ways to neutralize a dangerous situation. For example, often when the husband says, "I don't want to talk about this now. I need peace and quiet," the wife follows him around, nagging, until he explodes. During the meeting the wife can say, "Instead of hitting me, punch the wall; then I'll know I'm being provocative." Another strategy, which husbands love, is for the couple to agree beforehand that if she keeps provoking him he'll start taking off his clothes, starting with a tie or shoe and continuing until he's naked, no matter where they are—in a restaurant, friend's house, etc.—until she stops complaining. The wife is terrified of making a scene in public, so the nagging stops completely.

Violence is possible because it's secret. As soon as you reveal it, society has to intervene. If she can't understand what she does to provoke her husband's aggression, she should divulge what is happening to the elders—his parents, grandparents. The elders need to state: "This is just not acceptable." This divulging shouldn't be done behind her husband's back. She should warn her husband, "If you hit me again I am going to tell the extended family."

The bottom line is that a dangerous situation must be neutralized, not magnified. If the husband comes home and says, "The house is a mess," the wife can think, "You had a good time at work while I slaved with the children." But in the moment she needs to be calm and say, "I'm sorry dear. I'll clean everything tomorrow." When the situation stabilizes she can say, "Look. I need appreciation for the things I do around the house." But when his temper is hot she needs not to stoke, but throw water on it.

" MY TAKE "

The non-PC nature of Dr. Madanes's response will doubtless cause eyebrows to raise: "Are we going back to blame the victim?" But any input that can be helpful should be considered and not dismissed out of hand. The research of which she speaks is outlined in *Family Interventions in Domestic Violence: Handbook of Gender-Inclusive Theory and Treatment*, edited by John Hamel, LCSW, and Tonia Nicholls, PhD (Springer Publishing Company, 2006). The gist is that this is not a black-and-white issue; many complexities exist when it comes to partner violence.

It can never be said enough—nothing justifies violence! However, it might take the patience of Job to "yes dear" a mate as Dr. Madanes suggests while he is being accusatory. Perhaps it would be easier for the wife to leave the room, saying simply, "I don't want to fight. Let's talk about this later." The point is, when the husband is mad his spouse shouldn't make him angrier. Refraining from provocative behavior doesn't make her a patsy but a smart strategist.

People have to own their behavior, and as both experts assert, if the wife is allowing this to happen, especially around the children, that is tantamount to child abuse. I like Dr. Cohen's focus on not just triage but a "cure." The wife should seek therapy to understand why she has put herself in this situation as well as push the husband to anger management classes. If he cannot admit that his behavior is unacceptable and/or he will do nothing to prevent it, she must put the children first. This means asking herself, "Do I want to batter them by allowing them to see me being battered?"

As Dr. Cohen says, abusers strike their spouse in an effort to exert power. They need to feel in control in at least one area of their life. Even if this control is only infrequently expressed in a physical outburst—once is too much!—there are other signs that the relationship is abusive. For example, does the husband constantly insult, criticize, and make his wife feel stupid and unworthy? Does he tightly control the purse strings and/or need to know his mate's every move? Is he constantly flinging accusations of infidelity? These are dangerous precursors—insulting words and a possessive attitude can escalate to physical attacks.

Violence is a deliberate choice, not the result of an out-of-control rage. Men and women are both guilty of exhibiting abusive behavior toward their spouse. However, whether or not a wife exhibits behavior that could be construed as provocative, the fact is that women are more likely to be hurt by domestic violence than men. Indeed, of those murdered by their intimate partner, 74 percent are women.

Take advantage of services offered such as the National Domestic Violence Hotline

My wife is undergoing chemotherapy. I'm frightened she won't make it, but trying to be strong. Should I tell her how scared I am?

WILLARD F. HARLEY, JR., PhD:

Absolutely. I believe in a policy of "radical honesty." This is important for three reasons. First, dishonesty, keeping certain feelings to yourself, is what I call a "love buster." People don't like it if you don't tell them the truth. Second, honesty is an emotional need. When couples are radically honest, you get to the real truth. Third, being honest is the only way you develop a complete understanding of your partner.

So this husband needs to tell his wife he is frightened and doesn't want anything to happen to her. She might say, "I'm having enough trouble dealing with this. Don't tell me how you're feeling." That's fair . . . honest . . . and part of a great marriage.

If that's her response, then he knows his best move is to go for emotional support elsewhere and continue being strong for his wife.

BARBARA SWENSON, PhD:

It depends on the couple. Where is the wife in terms of her illness? Is she completely freaked out and unable to handle her husband's distress in addition to her own? In this scenario the husband sharing his feelings might make her feel less supported. On the other hand, in a healthier marriage she might welcome knowing he's scared also: "He understands how serious this is." Now they can both share their fear with each other and have a connection on that level.

Has he traditionally been the type who has not been very supportive? Do they have a long history of everything being all about him and his needs? The fact that he's asking this question, "Should I share my feelings?" shows sensitivity on his part toward his wife. He probably could admit to feeling scared and by her reaction sense if she perceives this knowledge as comforting or a burden.

It's about tuning in to each other's feelings.

" MY TAKE "

The experts have a small divide. Dr. Swenson says tune into your wife, intuit which way the wind is blowing and proceed from there. Dr. Harley advocates honesty at any cost. Anything shy of total truthfulness will harm the marital bond.

While one doesn't want to cause further upset to a spouse who is already suffering, as Dr. Swenson says, he or she wants to know you're affected as well. If you weren't, what kind of marriage would it be? However, ultimately I tilt in Dr. Harley's direction on this question—honesty perhaps not radically, but tactfully and carefully. Choose a time that feels particularly loving, and definitely not right before or after a chemo treatment. If you bottle up your feelings and act like a manservant at her total beck and call, unvoiced resentment will eventually uncork your lips and thoughtless words will fly.

Yes, the wife's needs are primary, but the healthy partner must take care of himself as well. The burden of caregiving is tremendous. In addition to having people to turn to for support, as Dr. Harley intimated, it is also imperative that the husband allow himself time to relax and self-generate. Keep the weekly bowling league date (barring an emergency, of course), buy that set of golf clubs you've been yearning for, and enjoy the simple pleasures of a good novel and junk food.

How can we keep our infertility from taking over the marriage?

STEVEN STOSNY, PhD:

Becoming obsessed about anything will detract from the relationship. Obsession means your brain has decided you can't be happy or well with each other unless you have the thing you're obsessing about.

There's a lot of disappointment. Sometimes there is anger and resentment toward the spouse. When you're in a powerless place it becomes easier to get irritable with your partner, to find something you don't like about what he or she is doing. Some couples in this position blame the doctor. It can be a temporary bonding experience—giving them a common enemy, but it's superficial. They'll eventually turn on each other.

Men and women deal differently with stress. Men tend to withdraw, while women want more closeness. Infertility is usually harder on women than it is on men. The husband needs to be really compassionate toward his wife. She in turn should be understanding, realizing that when he does withdraw it's a coping mechanism, not proof he doesn't love her.

Couples need to say they're in this together and be supportive of one another and understanding of successes and failures with fertility treatments. It's important to be able to accept that you can be happy and whole without having the object of your obsession—in this case, a baby. You're actually more likely to get the object of your obsession if you can develop this sort of Buddhist philosophy.

To get to that place you need to look at your core value. What is most important to you? Eventually you might come to see that what's most important is to be loving and compassionate toward the people you love. If you keep this in mind, it's easier to get through stressful times without taking it out on loved ones.

Many people have children in order to feel fulfilled. But in actuality, to be a good parent means you were happy before you had children. That way you won't put pressure on your child to make you happy. Being happy though childless is a better predictor of what kind of parent you will ultimately be and what kind of marriage you have.

Rebecca Roy, MA, MFT:

It's important for the couple to acknowledge unresolved issues such as grieving. Not being able to conceive involves feelings of loss of control, loss of self-esteem, and often financial strain. Fertility treatments don't come cheap. And make no mistake—men get just as upset as women over not having a child.

Commonly there is often sexual pressure around infertility, such as being compelled to have intercourse at certain times. To counteract this, make sure you are not just having sex for purposes of procreation. Shake things up a little. Vary the setting and sexual techniques. Otherwise sex gets reduced to "input" and "output," literally and figuratively.

Make an effort to reconnect by talking about what you value about the relationship—companionship, emotional support, activities you enjoy doing together. Start looking at what you have, not what you don't have. If the relationship is all about children, then the relationship will seem worthless. Take walks together, work out together, and—very important—get away as much as possible from family members who nag you mercilessly about having children. Be polite but shut them down: "It's something we really want. We're continuing to work on it. When anything develops we'll let you know."

" MY TAKE "

For many people, the desire to have a child is primal. And when fulfillment of that primal need is thwarted, self-absorbed childish impulses often come out to play, impulses which, according to Dr. Stosny and Roy, can wreak havoc on a marriage.

Dr. Stosny keys in on how any obsession is cancerous and all-consuming. When someone is so angst-filled, he or she looks to project that emotion outward, typically on the nearest available person—guess who? The expert stresses that the antidote to this vat of yearning and misery is to home in on one's inner Oprah. Be grateful for what you have together rather than bitter about what is lacking.

Roy takes that premise further, giving specific advice on how to reconnect: Don't make sex all about baby-making, and don't let crazy-making relatives pour fuel on the fire.

The experts are divided on how infertility affects both genders. Dr. Stosny is in the traditional camp that says women feel the pain more acutely. Roy feels the misery is shared. According to a 2007 study published in the *Journal of Marriage and Family*, women are more comfortable with the idea of childlessness than men. A reason cited is that men "experience strong economic and social rewards" for fatherhood, while for women child-rearing still means more pressure and responsibility on a day-to-day basis.

To take Dr. Stosny's point further, when tragedy strikes it is helpful to strive for a Buddhist rather than ruinous philosophy. Look on this difficult time as a challenge to rise above. Like the death of a child, infertility can be a make-or-break issue. But as the saying goes, what doesn't kill you makes you stronger. This is one of those "for better or worse" moments the couple pledged to get through in the wedding vows. Infertility is the foe; the partner is not. Sometimes one person will be more up to the task of handling the pain and disappointment than the other. The stronger mate should be there for the "weaker" one. When the more depleted partner has recharged, the positions can reverse. If each one can put the partner and the marriage first, if each one can say, "After getting through this we can get through anything," they will emerge with a rock-solid marriage.

While in the middle of a minefield, it is hard to imagine ever walking carelessly and gaily again. But it will happen. Even if the wife never gets pregnant, knowing they helped each other through this crisis can be a relationship-saving thread. Having things not go one's way can be regarded a gift. Not one that was chosen, granted, but a priceless opportunity nonetheless.

My husband of eleven years just confessed he's bisexual but says his occasional flings don't detract from his love for me. I'm shocked, devastated, mortified. . . . He wants to stay married. I love him but don't know if I can handle this. Help!

Stephanie Buehler, MSW, PsyD, CST:

The Internet has helped a lot of married bi people realize there are others like them out there. The issue becomes how to come out to their partner. Will the wife permit him to keep experimenting now that she knows? He's a nice guy, a considerate, loving partner, but he can't hold this in anymore.

This has to be negotiated carefully. The couple has to forge an agreement. He and the wife need to get tested. Is the husband going to be practicing safe sex? Is he going to have an ongoing relationship with someone else or just occasional flings? Can he go away for a weekend and just be gay once in a while? Do they have kids? Regardless, does the wife need her husband to commit to total fidelity?

There is often much guilt and shame around this. A woman shouldn't take it personally, but it can be hard not to. If the marriage has been good she can be pretty understanding that his orientation is bi, but what bothers her is the idea that he'd go outside the marriage for sexual gratification. To her bi usually means gay. Sometimes she can deal with his attraction to another woman, but it's very threatening for her to feel she has to compete with a man. She could more easily accept his just wanting to look at gay porn. How much control can she have over her partner's sexuality? She needs to talk to him in a non-blaming, nonthreatening way, which involves getting her fragile sexual ego out of the equation.

Ultimately, it's whatever feels okay. I've seen couples work it out where one partner is a cross-dresser, but frankly I've rarely seen this kind of arrangement survive after the coming out.

MICHELE WEINER-DAVIS, MSW:

I've worked with couples in long-term marriages where it comes out that the husband is gay or bi. It's challenging to keep a relationship together in this circumstance; very challenging, but it is possible. Both partners have to be committed to staying together and there must be clear guidelines and expectations with an extraordinary level of honesty.

First, there are health issues. If he's having sex elsewhere, it has to be safe sex. Then, what are the expectations about the wife's sexuality? Is she going to go outside of the marriage? How will they be able to talk about this with the children? What if the people outside the family find out—how will that be handled?

Regardless of how long the couple has been married, it might be hard for the wife to find peace with this information. She'll think: "How did I miss this? What does this say about my gut instincts?"

The straight spouse has to not take it personally. It's almost easier to find out your mate is gay than having an affair with someone of your own sex. Then it's not a comment on you, but on your husband's sexuality, which is determined by a number of factors, not including an unsatisfactory heterosexual relationship.

" MY TAKE "

Both Dr. Buehler and Weiner-Davis agree this is a heartbreaking dilemma the "solution" of which is often divorce. The experts also concur that if the goal is to stay together, guidelines must be established about exactly how this bombshell will express itself in the marriage. Clearly there is a difference between the husband scrolling through gay porn but otherwise staying faithful versus him being allowed occasional boys-only jaunts. There is also an accord here that if the wife can't move beyond taking her husband's sexual orientation as a personal rejection, she should invite him to move out of the house.

The sole bone of contention between the experts is which wounds a woman more—discovering her husband is attracted to men or that he is having an affair with another woman. While both are hurtful, obviously there is no clear-cut "winner." It depends on the woman and the particulars of her ego deconstruction. But pain is pain and in this scenario there are boatloads!

There are two very painful issues hitting this woman simultaneously: the ice-bucket-dunked-over-her-head discovery that her husband is bi, followed by the triple-ice-buckets-dunked-over-her-head discovery that he's been cheating. As with any spouse confronted with a partner's infidelity, she has a right to be angry, to demand answers as well as demand that her husband make it a priority to restore her trust. This means he must be transparent, and henceforth totally honest.

The husband is professing a disinterest in giving up his flings. If he remains intransigent even if it's a deal breaker, the wife has her answer on how to proceed. If after the shock wears off she feels there might be a way to save the marriage, what capitulations and guarantees are needed to make this arrangement feasible?

Therapy will be very helpful at this crucial juncture. But here is another, potentially invaluable resource that can provide a couple at this impasse with strength and information: the Straight Spouse Network (SSN; *www.straightspouse.org*). SSN is an international online organization that provides a conduit to support groups and offers research-based information and outreach about some of the unique issues faced by bi/straight couples. According to SSN, there are two million gay or bisexual people who either will marry or are already married.

FIELD REPORT

In twenty years of marriage the closest my husband and I got to breaking up was following the death of our son. We isolated instead of grieving together. Innocent comments were often misunderstood and caused us to further feel alienated. It was becoming more and more evident that we were going to split up. Then one day, I grasped that my husband was the only person in the world who had experienced the same loss as me. I told him that I didn't want our son's death to also cause our divorce. We decided to begin to grieve together. This realization came to us as an answer to our prayers. It became so much easier to be kind to each other and rebuild what we had lost.

~Kathy A. Eubanks, 46, Chesterfield, Michigan

FROM THE FILES OF . . .

Joyce Morley-Ball, EdD

The couple, in their forties and married six years, were each on their third marriage. This was not surprising, as the wife was controlling, while the husband admitted to being a philanderer. Each had children from previous marriages but none together. Each blamed the other for the impasse that had led to them being—the sole area of agreement!—on the verge of divorce.

The therapist's strategy was deceptively simple: "I told them, 'You can sit around blaming each other all day or look inside yourself to see what you've contributed to what's gone wrong in the marriage.'" This gave them permission to be human and admit to their imperfections, first to themselves, then to each other.

Over the course of the year they spent in therapy, they received regular homework assignments. For example, each was asked to keep a journal. The objective—to start seeing how their backgrounds impacted their present actions (i.e., the husband had learned infidelity was acceptable by watching his grandfather and father cheat on their wives; the physical and emotional abuse inflicted on the wife by her father left her needing to discharge a perennial anger toward men on the nearest target).

The therapist explains, "Once they started seeing their patterns, they could choose to do something different." Dr. Morley-Ball adds, "Six years after our counseling sessions ended, the wife still says that the therapy process was one of the best things to ever happen to them!"

CHAPTER NINE

DUELING GOALS

❧

When couples are in sync the two feel like they are working together for a mutual goal, such as having a child, buying a house, or saving for a vacation. When their priorities are not aligned, conflict and distance can swiftly arise. This chapter is about the disconnects; how to problem-solve when two people crave different things. What if only one spouse wants a child? What happens when one partner feels the other has become vapid and materialistic rather than caring about things that really matter? Those are some of the problems dealt with by the amazing marriage experts consulted on these issues.

My husband has gone from saying he wants kids someday to not being sure if he ever wants a child. I feel betrayed. What can I do to get him to change his mind?

Barbra Williams Cosentino, LCSW, RN:

You can encourage him to talk about his fears. Typically men are not very good at identifying the feelings that are getting in the way of knowing why they want or don't want to do something. So if he can identify some of those feelings, you might be able to find a back door to addressing those fears that are getting in the way.

There are many common fears that make a man ambivalent about having children. For instance, he may subconsciously fear that the wife will love the child more than she loves him. Or that having a child will turn her into his mother. Or that she'll start acting parental toward him—becoming nagging, critical, overprotective. Often a man becomes afraid he will no longer be sexually attracted to his wife once he's seen her in childbirth. Or that they'll never have sex again. Or that the wife will become so involved with the baby he will be pushed aside. Or that there will be a loss of spontaneity after the child is born. It won't be so easy to just pick up and go to the beach for the day.

The aim is to get him to acknowledge and discuss some of these fears without trying to counteract them. Don't have an agenda. If you push he might feel cornered and dig in his heels. What he needs is to have his feelings supported, not subverted. Understand that many of his fears may be a reflection of his childhood, which has colored his expectations of what he thinks a good father should be. Often, just thinking of becoming a father can stir up old conflicts that had seemed resolved.

If you remain at an impasse, seeking professional help is an option, as is punching a hole in your diaphragm—and yes, that last part was a joke.

DON AND MARTHA ROSENTHAL:

There is a profound difficulty in this situation. You should rephrase the question. Rather than trying to change the husband, which he could connote as a lack of respect for his feelings, ask, "How can I join together with him to come to a solution that works for both of us?"

You want to create an opening so that he feels validated. This involves being curious and asking questions to learn not just how he feels, but why he feels that way, and how strongly he feels it—everything you can find out. When one wife explored her husband's reluctance to be a father, he got past his fear and negativity and was able to share his worry over the financial restrictions this lifestyle change would cause. Reflect back what he says so your husband feels understood. If he feels "gotten," some of his defensiveness will soften and he will let you inside.

At this point you can ask him to try to understand as deeply as possible how you feel, how very much you want a child. He can reflect back what you say to show his understanding of your feelings.

The two of you can then agree to sit together in a place of "we don't know," where it's okay to not have an immediate resolution but to be open to supporting one another. The answer to the dilemma can come if there is a willingness to be informed from a deeper place of wisdom and love. You have to dive down beneath the rational mind and fear to get in touch with this meditative place. When two people of goodwill understand each other deeply, they can clear their minds, allow their thoughts to take a rest, ask for guidance, and sink down to this sacred place.

" MY TAKE "

The consensus here is that the wife should strive to make her husband feel understood, rather than guilted into feeling like a cartoon villain for disappointing his wife. To that end Williams Cosentino suggests helping him voice the reasons behind his seemingly sudden ambivalence. The therapist's proviso to "not have an agenda" while you pursue this task is dead-on, if difficult to accomplish while writhing with the dark emotions that accompany the belief that you've been betrayed.

The Rosenthals prescribe using this place of mutual understanding of one another's positions as a springboard to delve deeper into a place of trust, love, and hope that the answer can come. This spiritual exercise can be powerful indeed, immensely helpful for anyone who feels eternally stuck between two virulently divergent options. But it takes a willingness to let go and let faith carry the day. Paging your inner Buddha!

A dilemma of this emotional heft can really test a marriage. It is a make-or-break issue. Added to this division is the pain and anger the wife feels, rightly or not, at being misled or lied to.

There is no easy answer. As the experts noted, empathy is very helpful. The spouse did not come to his viewpoint to hurt his wife but because the thought of having a child feels so untenable. He should not be bullied into having a child. Nor can he expect that his wife's desire to have a child will fade over time.

Where does this leave the couple? In a pregnant place (forgive the pun), one of waiting to see if, over time, the strength of the pair's opposing feelings remains the same or is diluted. If that softening occurs—say, the husband comes to believe that losing his wife would be more of an unwanted jolt than adjusting to daddyhood—the couple might eventually become parents. But if he remains unswerving in his position, can she deal with never having a child? Whatever you do, don't poke a hole in that diaphragm!

Whenever my wife and I have a bad fight she says we should get a divorce. She later apologizes, but it makes me worry. When we got married I vowed to stay together no matter what. How can I make sure she feels the same way?

Alisa Ruby Bash, MA, MFTI:

It sounds like this wife is triggering her husband's abandonment issues. There's a bit of a sadomasochistic quality here. From the way he phrased the question, it seems he feels like the victim and she's more the victimizer.

This couple should talk when they are calm to discuss the pattern that's emerging in the way they are fighting. One person is trying to control the other by threatening to leave. In a time of calm they need to share how the idea of divorce makes them feel. Has it changed since they first got married? This is an opportunity to assess the relationship and how committed they are to it.

The partner who has been threatening divorce has a lot of bottled-up frustration. Is the couple open to the idea of seeing a marriage counselor? If they prefer to work things through on their own, it's advisable to set aside a weekly "check in" time where they can discuss issues that have come up.

Fighting is essential for healthy, long-lasting relationships, but they need to set up ground rules for fighting fairly. No hitting below the belt, no name calling or screaming or rudely interrupting the other person. To resist the urge to go on the attack, they should take deep breaths when their anger starts to take hold. At those moments it's important to remind themselves to really listen to and feel compassion for one another.

Bernard J. Baca, PhD, LCSW:

He can't make sure she feels the same way. She feels pretty much the opposite of what he feels. This is common in relationships. What this means is the husband has to understand and empathize with why she uses that line, "I want a divorce." It is rooted in her childhood dynamics. What happened to her growing up? My hunch is she often felt abandoned. The wife fell in love with him because he was confident and capable—the qualities she felt she lacked. It was probably like this in her family of origin and got transferred to her spouse. What she is doing now is beating him to the punch. She's not trying to hurt him but to protect herself. She feels, "There's something in me that is worthless."

The husband's core issue is, "I'm special but maybe not so special." Translation: He has narcissistic tendencies but underneath exist feelings of shame.

He will always be attracted to someone with abandonment issues, as she will look up to him. But inwardly he feels, "I'm good, but if you look hard enough I'm not good enough." Perhaps he had a depressed mom and his dad was unavailable and no matter what he did to take care of his siblings and parents, no one valued him as much as he felt he deserved. Now no matter how successful he is to the outside world, he doesn't feel successful enough. The wife threatening divorce triggers his childhood feelings of putting on a false self, the self that looks good to everyone but him and maybe his wife.

So what looks like a different place is covertly the same place. Both have abandonment issues and they found each other to "fix" these issues.

But she's not going to change first. He has to. He can do this by learning not to be so self-absorbed. When she threatens to leave he can say, "I hear you want a divorce. Tell me more about why." Often couples need a counselor to help them get to this place. It's the place where they can admit their vulnerability to the other. She wants to reach the soft spot beneath his competent core—not the superman persona. She wants to be heard, since she hasn't been truly heard her whole life. As that begins to happen she won't need to threaten divorce.

" MY TAKE "

The experts' conflicting answers pose a bit of a He Said/She Said. Bash sees potential sadomasochistic overtones via the wife's need to control and the husband's desire to be the victim while Dr. Baca views the impasse as driven by the husband's need to feel superior. To Dr. Baca, the wife's verbal punch comes from a feeling of abandonment, of not being heard, not mattering. According to Bash, the wife's outburst is the volcanic result of storing up too much emotional lava.

Both the husband and wife are fed by the same well—fear of abandonment—even if they come by that fear through different but equally wounding childhoods. And Bash's dictates for fighting fair are helpful for any couple to follow regardless of their individual issues and patterns.

The husband's plaintive question, "How can I make sure she feels the same way?" reeks of insecurity. Here's my riff: While the wife should work on not defensively launching into attack position whenever she feels overwhelmed and upset, there is no amount of reassuring she can give her husband that will make him feel "safe" in the relationship if at his core he feels unloved and unlovable. Perhaps his intense neediness makes the wife feel cornered and not good enough for being unable to fully relieve his anxiety. Thus her self-loathing helps trigger her attack on him, which triggers a bout of insecurity on his part.

So the pattern of beating each other up goes on, and will continue until both partners realize that they are locked in an old dance and determine to break out and learn some new steps.

My marriage used to be close and happy. Over the last six months I've noticed a change. It feels like my spouse has time for everybody and everything but me. How can I get him to view our marriage as a priority, something worth fighting for?

Michael D. Zentman, PhD:

The most important thing is to focus not on your partner but on yourself. Rather than accusing him—"Why haven't you been around lately?"—ask yourself, "What can I do differently?"

Express that you miss your mate in a way that doesn't sound blaming and see if your feelings are reciprocated: "It feels like we haven't been doing fun things together. Have you been thinking the same thing? Maybe we can go antiquing next weekend."

The idea is to approach the lack of couple time lightly and with humor, if there's still some left in the marriage! Act in a way that makes your partner want to be around you versus feel guilted into it. Strive not to sound demanding, as that can elicit a defensive response.

The most valued real estate in a marriage is the moral high ground, but owning that won't help your relationship. After all, very rarely is one person totally innocent; look to see what you've been contributing to the emotional distance. For instance, how much time do you spend on the Internet?

Put yourself in your mate's position. Might he view the emotional environment as toxic, expecting to be subjected to accusations, stonewalling, and/or contemptuousness from a spouse (you!) increasingly desperate for attention? Anything that can "warm" the environment and make him feel respected, understood, and cared about can reduce his sense of detachment from you.

It's very important that you don't complain to your friends that your spouse doesn't seem interested in you. It's nice to have support, but that can become corrosive to the marriage. It's something intimate you're sharing with someone other than your mate.

BARTON GOLDSMITH, PhD:

In some respects marriage is like an algebra equation—the two sides must be balanced. When one side changes considerably, the other side responds. By unilaterally acting loving toward your partner, you are taking away, to a large respect, his reason for moving away from you. For example, if your spouse initially withdrew feeling that whatever he put into the marriage wasn't being reciprocated, he is now being given a reason to move forward.

The North Star of a relationship is commitment. Ultimately it does take two people to "save" a troubled marriage. I've worked with couples where one or the other felt huge obstacles in the way, taking their attention away from one another. After three years of being at loggerheads, one couple's priorities completely realigned when the husband was diagnosed with cancer. The wife said, "Those petty things I've been holding on to don't matter." It needn't take such an extreme event to trigger this change. Often it's a letting go of the need to "win." Neither wants to be in the wrong. But you can be right or you can be happy.

" MY TAKE "

Dr. Zentman is all about numero uno, but not in an "I am the world" kind of way. His proclamation is: Get over yourself and how you've been wronged and focus on your partner. The aria isn't "I, I, I" but "What can I do for you, you, you." Make the environment pleasant and comforting. Would you want to spend time in a home where every time you walked in you cringed, thinking, "Ooops, incoming insult"?

Dr. Goldsmith's math lesson is that 1 plus 1 must equal 2. What if your partner's preferred addition is 1 plus 1 equals screw you? His suggestion to right the balance echoes the advice offered by Dr. Zentman. Make the happiness of your partner a priority. Dr. Goldsmith's rationale is that morphing into president of your mate's fan club might reawaken his dormant instincts to make you the center of his world. Dr. Goldsmith isn't stressing a reassessment of what has caused the marital rift, just a sharp turn of the wheel to hopefully right the balance. However, if the ship continues to list and the North Star permanently vanishes from the horizon, ultimately a reassessment might be in order.

I second Dr. Zentman's directive to keep it in the family. All that negativity you spill about your mate to others can boomerang and come home to roost, making that all-important environment that much more unloving and toxic.

The emphasis here on not apportioning blame or employing guilt tactics is sound, but there is a question that desperately needs answering. Until recently the partnership was close. Why has your mate pulled away? If you can stress that you're not asking with the purpose of then countering with a blast of defensive, ego-driven vitriol, but because you really want to listen, and to truly hear, the breach can begin to heal.

The rupture came about partially because your ears closed to one another. Perhaps you stopped hearing what you wanted to hear (such as approval and pronouncements of love), so your partner's words simply became noise. But being able to hear, without feeling threatened, where your partner is now—not six months ago—is a gift he will cherish. Often we shove the elements comprising our marriage into a box, thinking we know every inch of it so well it's not necessary to open the box very often and take a look.

People change and evolve. Back to the numbers. While the longed-for marital equation remains $1 + 1 = 2$, the 1s change over time. If the foundation of your relationship involves mutual commitment, the marriage won't be unduly rocked by expressions of individuality. Over the long haul two strong 1s make for a stronger 2.

I've never cared about possessions and status and my spouse has become this person I barely recognize—all about living large and entertaining vapid, wealthy people. We're becoming more and more estranged. Can we find our way back?

Frank Pittman, MD:

Couples don't just grow apart. They stop talking to each other about how life feels. They stop discussing their different ways of looking at things, and about what it feels like to be married. They stop showing curiosity about what it feels like to be their partner. You need to have a sort of split screen where you see not only what your life feels like to you, but how it feels to your partner as well.

The hardest couples for a therapist to work with are those who don't have curiosity. You have to live your life as a series of adventures which you then report back to your spouse.

I recommend to all couples that they read novels and go to movies that are about people having connections, not just car crashes. Otherwise that's what the relationship can become. A car crash.

WILLARD F. HARLEY, JR., PHD:

If this couple followed my rules for a few months, this problem would disappear.

Every decision must be made with enthusiastic, mutual agreement. The objective is to learn to negotiate on any issue, from how to raise the kids to what type of lifestyle the couple want to lead. There are four steps involved leading to the objective of a mutually agreed-upon goal:

Step One: The discussion has to be safe and enjoyable. A decision cannot be made until both partners feel good about it. So unless they want to remain in limbo, they need to make the discussion pleasant.

Step Two: Each must understand the other's perspective on the issue in dispute. You already understand your own, so you have to ask a lot of questions, and do so with a great deal of respect for your partner's way of seeing things. Don't think you can change his or her perspective. The idea is to work with that perspective in mind to achieve a mutual agreement.

Step Three: Brainstorm. You may not be able to think of a solution right away. Jot down ideas during the day. The point is to give yourself a chance to consider alternatives while you're sleeping. Your brain has an amazing capacity to work on problems without your awareness. The question is: How can both your interests be served by the final result?

Step Four: Reaching a mutual decision. This can involve a trial or a test. For instance, instead of picking up and moving to Manhattan, spend a week there first to see how you like it.

There is nothing wrong with either person's viewpoint. Discover the things you have in common; the intersections of common interest. You cannot continue behaving independently. Learn to develop a lifestyle that works for both of you and to make decisions with the other's interests in mind. Instead of arguing, search for common ground. There can be mutual sacrifice to achieve a common objective, but not one person sacrificing and one gaining at the other's expense.

" MY TAKE "

Will the movie of your life together be a tearjerker or a screwball comedy? Dr. Pittman's point that couples should expose themselves to films and novels that delve into relationships may initially seem like an indirect, albeit diverting, way of approaching a stressful dilemma. But it makes sense. Anything that serves to open a dialogue, to interject alternative viewpoints in a way that does not seem accusatory or loaded, is a tactic worth trying. It's when couples get locked and loaded into fixed, opposing positions that the slide toward marital fatigue begins.

Dr. Harley's four-step plan toward mutual, enthusiastic agreement more specifically focuses on having each acknowledge that his or her spouse's point of view is worth considering rather than summarily discounting it because it conflicts with a rabid self-interest. However, when a couple has reached the point of perilous estrangement, it can be hard to take that first step toward releasing the logjam.

A precursor to Dr. Harley's four steps is to spend a few hours together reliving the early days. A couple should ask themselves what first drew them together. They should share nostalgic memories that can trigger the feeling of life being "us against the world." Go back in order to ultimately move forward.

FIELD REPORT

Two years ago my wife and I were far apart. She dwelled on our financial problems. I just wanted to solve the problems. It felt frustrating, lonely, alienating. I felt disapproval of my wife and where she was placing her priorities. I knew if we didn't work out the differences between us there would be negative consequences for our marriage. So we began focusing on what we wanted for the relationship—mutual respect, friendship—rather than what we didn't want. Instead of blaming one another we said, "What can we do to support each other?" It took a while, many conversations, but we found a middle ground and feel joined again instead of distant.

~ Francisco J. Acosta, 44, Valley Stream, New York

LASTING LOVE

❧

Scott and Denise Gingold
Forks Township, Pennsylvania, married twenty-nine years

"Our respect for each other is unquestioning."

True, there were no bombs bursting in air when these two first laid eyes on one another in 1979. But there was a cacophony of ear-splitting sound. They met as volunteers for a rescue squad. Scott was the squad's captain and a self-described "bull in a china shop," while "nice, shy, and reserved" Denise was second lieutenant. Her duties included making sure everybody's uniforms were in order.

There were many midnight Scrabble games as the squad waited to be called out on emergencies. For two years the pair was *When Harry Met Sally* before the sex scene. They fell off the platonic bandwagon when a New Year's Eve date ended with a kiss. "We haven't stopped kissing since," says Scott.

They married in 1983. The groom was twenty-six, the bride twenty-five. Neither had previously been in a serious relationship or even knew what a good marriage looked like. Scott's father was five times divorced; Denise grew up with an abusive father. Her parents divorced when she was in college.

These difficult experiences left them determined to build a loving, respectful union.

Naturally, there have been times of struggle. They endured a six-year battle with infertility replete with genetic testing, daily hormone injections (Scott sticking his wife with a needle), and lovemaking morphing from spontaneously passionate to scheduled around Denise's ovulation cycle.

Scott says flatly, "Trying to have a child is one of the few things that can push a marriage over the edge."

As they were seriously considering in vitro, Denise became pregnant with Alex, now nineteen. Unfortunately the boy suffered from childhood asthma, allergies, stress, and migraines. Medical bills piled up.

Initially Scott worked as a salesman in the trucking industry. Denise was a physical therapist. "When there are trying moments you have to remember what drew you together in the first place," Scott says.

That ability came in handy when they started working together sixteen years ago in a management consulting company. Is it tough to be practically 24/7 companions? Scott's quick comment: "I get invited to boys' nights out all the time. I have no interest. I'd rather be with Denise."

Denise, not surprisingly, returns her husband's esteem. "When Scott is working he is so persistent and resourceful. I don't have that same aptitude. That's where you admire someone with qualities that are so opposite."

Scott leaps in to deliver the last compliment, on the "how great we work together" front: "She's a reflective thinker, someone who puts all the pieces together, while I just slam them in!"

The knack of working together quickly yet smoothly was essential when their son recently landed in the hospital for six days. Scott recalls, shuddering, "He had pneumonia aggravated by his asthma. The first few days were really terrible. Lots of question marks and trouble. Denise and I were in sync. At the same time I was texting a note to a doctor about the possibility of medevacking him to a better hospital, Denise walked in and said she'd come to that same decision."

Happily Alex recovered and resumed the frenzied life of a normal teen whose job it is to occasionally bust his parents' chops.

Those older folks each express the sentiment that should anything happen to the other, there will be no remarriage for the survivor. "No way I'd be with anyone else!" Scott affirms.

Friendship, determination, being in sync, constant communication—all valuable qualities for a couple to possess. But the super Krazy Glue that keeps *this* couple together is an unswerving mutual respect. Scott admits, "With other girls I got away with whatever I wanted to pull. From the beginning Denise never let me get away with anything."

He has a theory about why his wife was and is attracted to him and only him. "I'm cute as hell!"

CHAPTER TEN

ALL WORK AND NO PLAY

B eing a two-career couple involves, to a certain extent, becoming skilled circus performers. It's a high-wire act, a constant juggling of home and work duties. To add to the stress is the lack of agreement that couples, particularly those with children, often experience in parceling out said home duties. Thus it was essential to recruit an immensely talented team of marriage experts to answer questions about these complex dilemmas, ranging from how to finesse a long-distance relationship to handling the intricacies of running a business together.

Is there a way to keep from drifting apart when we spend more time with our work families than with each other?

JOHN BURKE MEALY, PhD:

Yes. This situation is similar to kids spending more time with their day care providers than with parents. The difference is that parents typically provide a whole lot more to their children in the time they do have together.

The marriage should be the number one priority. Make time every day—even if it's just fifteen minutes—to renew your bond with some intimate conversation and touching. At certain times it can be sensual touching, but sometimes it's utilizing stored body memories. Touching your partner's hand can reactivate deep bonding. If you're touching or revealing details of your private life to a coworker, that's dangerous territory.

The concept of dating should be continued into the marriage. You've got jobs, kids, and there are always chores. That's why fifteen minutes daily of committed time to one another is powerful. It's when couples take each other for granted that the need for closeness and intimacy is frustrated and the door opens to the idea of a workplace connection.

KATHRYN JANUS:

No one ever said on their deathbed, "I wish I had worked more." A relationship is a living entity. There is you, your mate, and this third thing. If on a conscious level couples don't make the relationship a priority, it will atrophy. They will be left with a parallel relationship, which is two partners leading separate lives, coming together to discuss household matters, things regarding the children, or making large purchases.

They must set aside time for each other, even if that time is allocated far in advance. This can be anything from booking season tickets to a theater company to setting an alarm to wake up early to have sex. Some couples say, "We want to be spontaneous." Which is better—being perennially too busy or tired to have sex, or doing it on a schedule? A physical connection is vital in a relationship.

If the pull of work takes precedence, regard that as an important symptom of problems in the relationship. Clearly the relationship is painful. Given the choice, couples will choose a place where they feel confident and appreciated over a place fraught with arguments and tension. In this case it's important to find out what you're avoiding in the marriage and why work has become an exit to intimacy in the relationship. That doesn't just mean sex, but connection.

Don't wait too long to do this work. Sometimes couples wait years before finally going to a counselor's office. By that time they're so disconnected that the task of reconnecting becomes really daunting.

" MY TAKE "

The verdict is in. The relationship must be a priority or it will "atrophy," as Janus cautions. I like her suggestion to start viewing a marriage as something separate—alive, delicate, and in need of constant nourishing. Also pay heed to her warning that if a spouse is more drawn to the work family than the nuclear one, there is serious trouble in paradise, trouble that should be attended to sooner versus later.

Dr. Burke Mealy's suggestion to devote fifteen quality minutes a day to one another is a wonderful starting point. However, don't take that as license to ignore a spouse the remaining twenty-three hours and forty-five minutes. If possible, take little breaks during the day to stay in touch—send a text saying, "Can't wait to hear how your talk with boss went," or e-mail a joke he or she will find funny. While work is front-burner during the day, a marriage partner should not be frozen out 'til evening.

Studies point to dual earners typically not using their jobs as a way to escape from family life; indeed, they are frustrated that they have so little leisure time together. Here are some tips for making the most of what little time there is to spend together:

- Shut out the world. That means no texting, e-mailing, or taking calls.
- If one partner is shouldering more of the domestic responsibilities when both are home, have a conversation about how the other partner can take over some of those tasks.
- Try to have at least one meal a day together. Don't be total ships in the night.
- It's easier to get through the daily grind if there's something to look forward to, such as the occasional night or even weekend away.
- Offer regular reassurances that your spouse is a priority. It never hurts to hear that one is valued!

We're about to start a business together. How can we handle being together 24/7 without killing one another?

Alisa Ruby Bash, MA, MFTI:

My first tip—avoid being in business together. It will put a strain on the relationship. However, if you're intent on going through with this plan, it can work if you set up ground rules and boundaries from the beginning.

Before you start, dip a toe in the water. Perhaps take a business trip together to woo a potential major investor and see how you work together. How does it feel to have a marriage partner as a business partner? At least one of you should continue to have another source of income. That will help alleviate stress.

Create defined roles for each of you based on your individual strengths. Try to respect each person's role in the business. It's also important to create personal space. You both need some privacy. Maybe a few days a week, one of you can work outside the home with a laptop. It's also crucial to maintain outside friends and interests. Couples can become enmeshed when living and working together, and you want to do what you can to not quash the passion between you. At a certain time of day make it a point to stop discussing business. Have playful time together as a couple.

Respect one another. If you get angry, take a second and walk away. You don't want to blow up at your partner. Look at the relationship as the most important thing. If working together causes the marriage to suffer, take a step back and reconsider. This is where it's important that you took the precaution of ensuring at least one of you maintained an income stream apart from the business.

Living and working with your best friend can be exciting. You don't know if this is something that can suit the two of you until you try. But the underlying rationale must be that the relationship is the most important thing.

John Curtis, PhD:

One of the major reasons couples get divorced is around the area of equity in terms of chores and division of labor. Many men still come into the relationship thinking of roles based on gender. How would it feel if you started a business together and it felt like your spouse wasn't pulling his weight? Resentment can contaminate love. It can also color the roles each person has in the business. Say she's the one with the head for numbers, but his gender bias leads him to think he's the one who should handle the money. This is something to be explored.

Both of you should write out job titles—office manager, sales manager—and come up with umbrella descriptions of what those titles mean. Sit down and ask, "Is there going to be a CEO or CFO? Will we be co-managers?" The ideal is to figure out titles and duties based on competency, not gender roles. Will there be multiple roles? Will you hire people as the company grows? Outsource? All functions should be listed.

How will all this change the duties in terms of the marriage and the home? Who will handle which personal task? Make a detailed list: Who walks the dog, shops for groceries, and the like?

Look at things from the macro level: Sit down like corporate executives and decide your long-term goals. For example, do you want to work hard and sell the business in ten years? Examine the micro level as well, the nitty-gritty: Who orders business supplies? The more thorough and prepared you are, the better your chances of success.

" MY TAKE "

Clearly, sinking heart, time, and dollars into a business venture is risky business. Both Bash and Dr. Curtis are emphatic that working together can be perilous to your relationship. If the decision is nonetheless made to live on the edge and become co-entrepreneurs, heed the experts' advice to carve out specific roles in this joint endeavor.

Dr. Curtis is dead-on about how gender biases still color our perception of how marital roles should break down. Biases can lead to simmering resentments that can add murky motives just when the couple desperately needs clarity to navigate this brave new world.

Bash's warning that at least one person have money coming in during the start-up period is beyond brilliant, as is her entreaty to not forget that the first order of business, no matter what happens to the fledgling company, is not to let the relationship suffer.

According to a 2006 U.S. Census Bureau survey, approximately 25 percent of all businesses are family owned. So clearly, despite the hurdles, many couples are making working together work. And to turn the gender bias on its head (or at least on its side), here's a fun fact: Women now hold 59 percent of all college degrees, and are making deep inroads into "male" fields such as computer science.

Back to the hurdles. As a further safeguard, instead of just outlining the roles each person will play, consider the suggestion of Rhonda Abrams, author of *The Successful Business Plan*. Write a partnership agreement. The purpose of the business plan is to hash out those nuggets that are not easy to talk about but crucial to discuss, such as who owns what percentage of the business and what happens to the business if the marriage ends.

If one spouse "works for" the business—just helping out rather than coming in as a co-manager—define the "employment" terms, such as pay, time off, and ability to quit. Understand how divorce laws can affect the future of the business. In community property states, the business may need to be sold or closed to divide the assets.

My husband just got offered a great job 3,000 miles away. The kids and I can't possibly follow, but I can't deny him his dream. Do all long-distance marriages necessarily fail?

JOHN BURKE MEALY, PhD:

Long-distance marriages are a challenge. Entering one is not something to do lightly. This couple should use a template to evaluate whether this arrangement can work for them. Will this be win-win? If it is win-lose—he's okay, she's not, or vice versa—it's a bad deal. The couple needs to keep negotiating until they create that win-win scenario. The husband has to have the same priorities as the wife or the marriage will be disturbed. And if the wife in the end says okay, but feels she'll be shouldering most of the burden with the house and children, she'll be weighted down with resentment. Compromises need to be made. Perhaps the wife and children will one day move to where the husband is going. He will set up the nest and when she arrives, her partner will do an extra load of child care while she pursues higher education or a new job. These negotiations are complicated and can't be squeezed into a short time frame—say, the two weeks his employer has given him to make the decision. This situation can be an acid test of the relationship. Sometimes you have to decide what is more important—getting your way or staying married.

Long distance obviously limits the type of communication between couples. People have needs—some sexual, some for intimacy and companionship. They should take the time and trouble to get together regularly, maybe every weekend, maybe once a month. There can be some visual input in between with web cameras and pictures. Send flowers, cards, items that are visually stimulating. And speak regularly to maintain an auditory connection.

Couples usually don't do long-distance relationships indefinitely but rather for a period of time, even if it's a few years. And they do it thoughtfully, without naiveté.

ELLA LASKY, PHD:

It's not a simple question. The couple has to talk about how all the roles will shift. How will the husband maintain his relationship with his children? Will he call at the same time every night to talk about their day, homework? Will there be a second call to check in with his wife? How often will he be able to come home?

Essentially the couple must set up rules. Men and women have different expectations. The husband will be lonely in another part of the country. Can he hang out with female coworkers? Can the wife hang out with male coworkers?

This arrangement is analogous to the husband going off to war and the wife remaining on the homefront and on duty 24/7. There are lots of practicalities. How will they handle their finances? When the husband comes home to visit does she relinquish the new roles she's taken on? It's not seamless to go back and forth between being mom and dad, and then just mom. It's an adjustment every time.

This wife already has worries about how this arrangement would potentially play out. Every decision comes down to assessing pros and cons. These should be aired in a respectful way. Once the decision is made, build in time to think about what's going well and what parts need to be tweaked. You're not going to get it right immediately.

" MY TAKE "

The consensus is this type of relationship is a risky proposition and both spouses need to be in accord on exactly how things will play out. Dr. Burke Mealy stresses that the couple should "negotiate" their way into a workable compromise in which no one feels shortchanged, or at least feels that way only temporarily. The marriage counselor also highlights that it is essential during a lengthy separation to maintain an intimate connection that, while hampered by the inability to touch, stimulates as many of our senses as possible.

Dr. Lasky brings up the touchy point that rules and boundaries must be set and enforced. How much contact is allowed with members of the opposite sex, and exactly what senses will such contact involve? And, points out the therapist, expect the arrangement to need constant attention, tweaking, and rethinking, just as would a healthy, ever-evolving marriage between cohabitants.

According to the Center for the Study of Long Distance Relationships (*www.longdistancerelationships.net*) in 2005 approximately 3,569,000 married persons in the United States reported they live apart for reasons other than marital discord. That translates into 2.9 percent of all marriages!

Research conducted by the Center indicates that one of the most important things long-distance couples can do to maintain an intimate connection is to live separate lives. This doesn't offer license to sleep around. Couples in long-distance relationships are no more likely to be unfaithful than are couples sharing the same bed. Rather, it's crucial to put effort into being social as well as engaging in activities that add a sense of productivity and meaning. This gives the couple more to share with each other when they do connect. Two half-persons do not a healthy relationship make; both partners should be complete, functioning human beings.

Along with the facet of being happy apart comes the sharing of the little and large details that happen day to day. This keeps a couple actively involved in each other's successes and struggles. The Center suggests utilizing technology to stay in frequent contact. Some couples carry hand-held recorders to "chat" into, and then send to their partner. Or couples can chat via hands-free cordless phones as they go about their day. As Dr. Burke Mealy suggested, others use cameras to transmit images of themselves doing everything from laundry to food shopping to giving a lecture to a packed auditorium.

It's easy to take one another for granted when you live together. The upside of being apart is that it gives you the opportunity to really appreciate each other.

FIELD REPORT

We each have our own small business. Very demanding of time. But as it's a second marriage for both of us, we are each aware that the marriage has to come first. We make sure to get out together away from work even if it's just for a few hours. We're the ones at the restaurant who will be the cutups turning the music up too loud and making up stories about all the people around us. Work hard. Play hard. Always appreciate each other.

~ Glenn Phillips, 44, Birmingham, Alabama

IF I HAD A DO-OVER

Tomi Tuel
Sacramento, California

"Don't ignore warning signs of trouble ahead."

I got married at twenty-five. I'd just graduated from college and figured this was the next step. I thought, "This is a corporate guy." It seemed like he had a lot of potential. But while we were engaged he dropped out of school and went into construction. It felt like a bait and switch.

It was a soulless marriage and relatively sexless, considering how young we were. I was working full-time, going for my master's degree, raising our two kids. He kept making very bad business decisions so I had to work two jobs to get us out of a financial hole.

Ten years ago, when I turned thirty-three, my husband left me for someone else, a woman who worked at my company. It was humiliating, horrible. They flaunted it in my face.

I still would have stayed together despite the affair. My parents have been married fifty-one years. I was obviously unhappy but committed. My husband and I tried to make it work for three days, and then he went back to the other woman.

It took me a good year to come out of the haze. I saw a counselor, and laughing with my friends was very therapeutic.

To say my husband wasn't the right choice would be to negate my two children, so I won't go there. But I'm happily remarried for five years, while my ex is on his fourth wife and unemployed.

I'm at peace with my past mistakes. Things happen for a reason.

CHAPTER ELEVEN

IN GOOD COMMUNICATION WE TRUST

❧

S cratch a bad marriage and you'll likely uncover a case of poor communication. Whether it's a spouse futilely wishing his or her partner was a mind reader, the pair becoming enmeshed in a pattern of withdrawal and/or arguing, or partners consistently feeling misunderstood and devalued, couples need help, and need it fast, to understand the patterns behind the ways they interact together and create a healthier dynamic.

The dilemmas addressed by the marriage counselors consulted for this chapter include the world of hurt arising when a spouse cannot say "I love you" and the seemingly unalterable pattern of small disagreements turning into major battles.

How can we stop being so bored?

PHIL KIRSCHBAUM, LCSW:

A lot of couples are running on history: We were exciting once. It's as if those things were supposed to carry them indefinitely. Couples have to forge ongoing adventures that will help them create new historical markers that define their relationship. Some couples do nothing but sit in a restaurant across from each other and have minimal conversation. Go to a controversial movie or play; it will open up avenues of discussion. To the same end, check out local newspapers for weekend happenings around town that might be even remotely interesting.

If one or both partners are resistant to trying new things, I'd be interested to explore what old issues might be causing blocks. One person might be feeling in some way unappreciated and undervalued, so isn't willing to try an activity suggested by his or her mate. Is there a deal that needs to get worked out? If I'm gonna stretch and do something uncomfortable for me, are you willing to do some things that are of interest to me? Can we find something of interest to both of us?

LAUREN H. ZANDER:

Often each person is pointing the finger at the other for making things boring. But it's not just what your spouse is or isn't doing. What about you? Choose an ingredient or two to get romance going—maybe a candle-lit shower. Is that so hard?

The point here is that couples give up on having great agendas. They have everything they want. Things get boring when they're not chasing something. The pair is amazing on the buildup toward getting married and becoming established—buying a house, having children. Then it's, "Uh-oh. We're stuck in this house with kids. Now what?" They're spoiled.

The solution to being bored is to always work toward achieving something as a partnership. It could be getting good at ballroom dancing, or both going on a diet. You're a team. It's not one person waiting for the other person to initiate; it's your turn! Yes, it's nice to have equality but in the end, who cares? This is your life. Don't be so into things being fifty-fifty. "Shouldn't he? Why me?" That can kill a relationship. Isn't it better to make your relationship fun?

" MY TAKE "

The message passionately set forth by both experts is that excitement comes to those who create it. Kirschbaum rightly points out that many couples think that since they made an effort to stay fresh and exciting back when cavemen walked the earth, they can coast the rest of their lives. Not so.

Zander's advice is potentially marriage-saving. If one has a tit-for-tat mindset, constantly weighing everything from whose turn it is to take out the trash to whose turn it is to initiate sex, he or she will turn into someone who puts more energy into holding grudges than into creating something of beauty and joy. Sure, it's fun to feel entitled and sit back and let a spouse do all the work, but face it—he or she is probably feeling the same way. Stalemate.

Spouses share a home and children, but are they friends as well? Do they share stories about their day-to-day lives, do gym classes together, belong to a monthly book club? Studies have found that couples who are happiest are those who partake in challenging and fun activities together. While it's superlative if a couple is inspired to train for a marathon or volunteer at a soup kitchen, the equation needn't be doing a huge joint project or nothing at all. Sweat the small stuff. Well, not necessarily sweat, unless that's what the activity calls for. But make it a priority to regularly schedule in time for fun, be it playing Scrabble or mahjong, reading to one another in bed, or having a Sunday ritual of preparing French toast and Bloody Marys.

Another component of a couple's anti-boredom program is to not take each other for granted. Wives and husbands shouldn't treat each other like a comfy chair—sinking into it when the urge strikes, otherwise not giving it a thought. Be courteous and respectful versus figuring, "Oh, he/she has to put up with me for life. If I'm rude or moody, so what?" Go further—once every week or two give a little surprise. Bring her flowers just because; download that new Springsteen CD he's been itching to hear onto his iPod. Keep him or her always wondering, "What fun new thing does my amazing spouse have planned for me next?"

My husband never says he loves me, even though I've told him I need to hear the words. He says I'm too needy and I should know how he feels. Who's right?

LINDA OLSON, PSYD:

It's not a question of who's right or wrong. He's being unkind and unloving by dismissing and negating her need for positive reinforcement. It's very blaming to call his wife needy. That makes her feel unheard and unloved. Successful relationships are about being reciprocal and balanced.

A couple must learn to give and take. It's not a negotiation, but about each person being willing to honor and respect the needs of the other and to value the relationship above all else.

They need to create a "space" where it is comfortable to dialogue openly about their needs and how to get them met. The wife should help her husband feel safe enough to talk about why he feels uncomfortable using those all-important words. Perhaps he's not verbal and just can't bring himself to say "I love you." She can say she understands, and he can ask what else she needs to feel loved.

JOHN GRAY, PHD:

She's right. The husband thinks his wife should automatically know how he feels. But for a woman, hearing "I love you" is analogous to a man's need to have sex. How would he react if she said, "Why do you need to have sex again? We did it yesterday."

It feels good for her to hear words of love and romance, as it does for a man when he is paid for work. In her case the stress-lowering hormone oxytocin gets produced. Oxytocin doesn't have the same effect in a man. When he feels successful, testosterone levels perk up. Once a couple understands the biology, it can help them understand their differences and needs. For instance, a man "lives" on the left side of the brain, the talking, action-oriented side. He's not on the right side of the brain, where feelings are located.

Perhaps the couple can come to solutions that satisfy both. Since action is how he expresses feelings, they can agree on one, maybe a hug, that symbolizes "I love you." He can ask, "How about I come and find you and give you a hug?"

Additionally, she might suggest actions for him. He could buy little cards that say "I love you" and leave them around—in the silverware drawer, the car—for her to stumble on. When she locates one, it will be a sure oxytocin stimulator. A testosterone stimulator for him is if she exudes an attitude of appreciation when he performs one of these actions. That is much more beneficial than complaining and criticizing that he doesn't show her his love enough!

So a wise woman interprets her man's love by his actions, and a wise man realizes that all actions and no words is not always enough for his wife.

" MY TAKE "

I feel the love in these on-point answers. Husbands should take heed from Dr. Olson's point that dismissing a wife's neediness makes her feel alone and unloved rather than part of a team. I also like Dr. Olson's suggestion that the wife should make it safe enough for the husband to discuss why he won't deliver that oxytocin booster. Perhaps she can accomplish that feat by saying something empathetic like, "I know you want to make me happy, but saying those words isn't something that is easy for you. I'm not putting you down for that or trying to make you say them. I just want to understand why it's so tough."

Dr. Gray's explanation of the science behind what men and women need is extraordinarily helpful. Neither sex is better or worse than the other. We're just hard-wired differently.

With absolutely no intent to refute the sage advice offered by Dr. Gray—women are indeed the feeling creatures—I believe that many men need more than sex to feel cared about. I've had husbands confide that they wish their wives would occasionally be the one to be assertive about demonstrating love. Reminder to Venus: Testosterone-fueled creatures prefer those demonstrations be delivered via actions, not voicing the L-word.

Sometimes a woman, enmeshed in despair over her unmet need to wrest proof of deep emotion from her taciturn spouse, and feeling neglected and resentful, forgets that her mate wants and deserves to receive symbols of love. She is not getting her due, thus oblivious that he is not getting his either. Indeed, if she performs thoughtful, concrete gestures for her mate—such as buying him tickets to a football game—he will respond by feeling loved and loving and perhaps even occasionally burst forth spontaneously with those three words.

Why does every small disagreement turn into a big fight that leaves one or both of us feeling hurt, angry, and/or massively misunderstood and unappreciated?

DEBRA MANDEL, PHD:

One or both of you are straying way beyond the environs of the initial disagreement, and indiscriminately feeling attacked and consequently defensive. This reaction commonly happens when we project negative intentions onto our partner: "Oh, he said that because he purposely wants to hurt me." That's not necessarily true. He probably said the comment you're deeming as hurtful because he's pained or confused.

Take a deep breath and try to ascribe positive intentions to your spouse. The two of you are likely reacting from old emotional wounds that have not healed from your families of origin. These wounds become reactivated in love relationships. It's easy to get angry and defensive when those feelings are unconsciously directed at your mother, father, siblings, and so on. Tell yourself, "My husband is not my brother, who had to beat me at every activity. He's just giving me constructive criticism on my tennis swing."

I teach couples to constantly keep that insight in their heads: "When I'm arguing with my partner I'm arguing with someone from my history as well." They need to realize this defensiveness is about needing to be genuinely heard, and feeling judged and misunderstood.

Ideally a couple can talk about these defensive tendencies in a time of calm so they'll have an awareness of what is being triggered. Then when your partner becomes upset at a later time you can say, "I see you're really angry. What am I doing to push your buttons?"

The two of you need to go beneath the surface argument to the historic feelings it triggers. If you can understand these core needs, you are home free.

Keith Ablow, MD:

Small disagreements reflect deeper issues between the couple. What seems like a skirmish about who is going to do which chore around the house can really be about whether a person feels valued in the relationship. Since couples don't commonly spend enough time discussing those real issues, displaced emotions pop up in unexpected places with more energy than we might expect.

A comment by the husband that he feels the couple is spending a little too much money could lead to a major battle if what his wife hears is another attack, more confirmation that her intelligence and autonomy are not respected by her spouse. This reaction will be even more heated if she never felt regarded as responsible in her nuclear family. In such an instance, feelings that have been intensifying for years, even decades, percolate upward.

The couple needs to develop what psychologists call a "third ear." This means working to achieve some kind of observer's

position that gives you emotional distance, enabling some perspective. This perspective is attained by asking questions even as
an argument unfolds. This is so much more powerful than making
statements. For instance, ask, "Why do we become so heated over
why you forgot to pick up rye bread on the way home? I want to
understand why we're tearing each other apart."

Suggest a ten-minute coffee break from the fight to sit down and
decipher together the root of the anger. Tell your partner, "I'm willing
to listen." Even if you don't feel fully able to put aside your hurt, your
partner will appreciate the attempt. Trying to understand someone's
position rather than being reactive is seen as an act of kindness, which
will likely be reciprocated and take you to a new place.

" MY TAKE "

The consensus: Check your ego and inner child at the door. Both Dr.
Mandel and Dr. Ablow speak about the human tendency to make
everything about . . . well, us! The smallest complaint ("Why didn't
you pick up bread?") can mushroom into a battle royal, which is a
loss for both sides no matter how it resolves. The more people can
separate from the history of hurts and victimizations they've been
carting around from childhood and concentrate on the here and
now, the better that here and now will be.

I endorse the suggestion offered by both therapists to choose
a time of peace and relative happiness to tackle a discussion about
what Dr. Mandel called these "defensive tendencies." But the suggestion worth the price of admission is Dr. Ablow's ten-minute coffee
break from the fight during the fight. If a mutually agreed-upon
détente can usher in a spirit of curiosity versus flinging accusations
of causality, both partners can become empathetic, a precursor to
understanding and bonding.

The three most powerful words one can utter to one's spouse
are not "I love you" (important as those are), but "I'm really sorry."
Nothing will puncture his or her anger faster than the sheathing of

claws. The apologizer may not agree with what his or her partner is saying, but no longer finds it crucial to vehemently press a self-righteous position. Apologizing, withdrawing from a quickly escalating, negative situation is a win for the partnership. If one "side" can lay down arms before drawing blood, it can induce the other to do the same.

Why can't she ever just let anything go—especially when I want to reconnect after a fight and make overtures to her?

Karen Sherman, PhD:

Biologically the brains of men and women are very different. Women process information in both hemispheres. The neurons are constantly lit up, giving the sense that women are holding on to things all the time. Men process information in either the right or left hemisphere, making them better at compartmentalizing. They can let things go more easily.

Once a husband understands this, hopefully he will realize that not responding to his wife won't make her go away. Her upset will continue, so he has to address the situation. This means listening, saying something like, "I see this really bothers you." He doesn't have to agree with her, but he should help her feel validated rather than dismissed.

What makes this difficult is that her anger toward him can propel her into attack mode. However, he should do his best to hear her out. If not, she'll continue to vent. If she continues going on and on, his best move is to say, "I've been listening for fifteen minutes. I'm a guy, so I'm having a little trouble holding on to everything you're saying." This should make her at least feel heard.

As we come to better understand the differences between the sexes, we will see that our not doing certain things isn't because we don't love our partner. We're just different.

Bernard J. Baca, PhD, LCSW:

I'd like the husband to think a bit more about what's going on with his wife. Rather than wishing she would jump through hoops to accommodate his need to move on, he needs to develop compassion for the little girl in his wife, the person who feels she's had to crumble her internal needs and adapt to external requirements. Likely she's tried to assert herself her entire life and someone would be bullying and she'd apologize and knuckle under. She married someone who treats her the same way. Now she's trying to grow away from that dynamic.

She fell in love with him because he was logical and linear, and he fell for her because she could express emotions. As time passed, he became angry that she's all emotion, and she felt anger that he's a machine. Their tasks are to bring out in each other the parts of themselves they've been repressing instead of attacking one another for possessing a part the other lacks.

To further explain—both of their adult personalities are defensive adaptations of childhood wounding, and the marriage is a repetition of childhood and emotional patterns. They married someone who reminded them of their parents. Consequently, they both love and hate the partner. They have to change their personalities if improvement is going to occur in the relationship. The only way to do that is to value their partner as much as they value themselves. This is unconditional love. When the husband develops empathy for his wife his own defensiveness will drop away. Currently this husband is operating from the stance of, "As soon as you get to know me you'll find something rotten and abandon me." So what he hears when she goes on and on is, "You're not so nice. You're self-centered."

They need to move away from their mutual self-absorption. It starts and ends with developing true empathy for the other person. When you love unconditionally you no longer see your spouse as your father or mother; thus the need to be defensive is gone.

" MY TAKE "

This question has elicited two very different perspectives.

Dr. Sherman's approach is more literal, straightforward. Men and women are wired differently. The husband should understand that the wife needs to spout her feelings and it behooves him to listen for as long as humanly (on the man curve) possible. Then he should inform her he's done listening. She must cease and desist. This advice sounds great in theory but as many couples can attest, it can be hard to manage without supervision. It would help if the husband would strive for an open mind while listening to his spouse, rather than evince the attitude he's under a dentist's drill. His wife has a point, at least to her mind, so it should matter to him.

Which brings us to Dr. Baca—who is on the all-empathy-all-the-time station. The therapist stresses that what brings couples together is the subconscious need to repeat childhood patterns by marrying someone who brings out the worst in them. The head-butting will continue until the couple develops an awareness of their dynamics and works together to help each other move beyond their dysfunction. Again, not an easy task, but an immensely rewarding one.

Holding on to grudges, needing to continually tally up points on the Who's at Fault board—Yes, I did this bad thing, but you were so much more childish (vindictive, stupid) when you did that—takes a lot of energy. Needing to be right or needing to be the victim or needing to secretly seethe but pretend all is forgiven (this husband's stance, perhaps?) might seem like justifiable positions, but they're not healthy ones. Do the reasons behind the "fights" change, while the emotions churned up by each new disagreement remain constant? Pay attention to that inner turmoil. That's what's important, not who left the toothpaste cap off the tube. Couples need to use that as a springboard to create a new way of relating. One that may not be as dramatic, perhaps, but who really wants to reprise the Battling Bickersons?

Why can't he just open up to me and tell me what he's thinking?

WARREN FARRELL, PhD:

For the same reason you can't open up to him. Both of you are afraid of saying something that can be perceived as critical. Your partner becomes defensive, an argument ensues, and the price paid for expressing one's feelings is greater than the satisfaction gleaned from sharing innermost thoughts.

It's also harder for a man to share secrets because for him the stakes are higher. Women have other outlets for communicating, but men tend to put all their emotional eggs in one basket. So his dependency on your approval makes him even more vulnerable.

More bad news: Women are worse than men at handling personal criticism. And since women have better verbal skills, they're better at attacking back and thinking of reasons why everything is really the guy's fault.

Most people would give an arm or leg to save their partner's life. Yet they can't listen without becoming upset. Want your partner to open up? Take a deep breath. Tell yourself, "This isn't about me. It's about him and what he needs." Give him a safe environment to express his feelings—a gift rarer than diamonds—and he'll begin to express them.

HARVILLE HENDRIX, PhD:

Your husband is anxious that if he makes himself vulnerable he will be hurt. When this has been a person's experience with intimacy growing up, he or she will likely choose a partner who activates the same childhood fears.

Freud called this behavior the repetition compulsion. What happened in the past is neurotically re-created in the present. We are set up to go with familiarity rather than something new. The trauma of childhood becomes the trauma of a marriage. Once you find someone who will give a different response than the parent, the unconscious can repair itself.

Here's how it works. On an unconscious level two people are brought together to help each other heal. In order to satisfy those needs that were left unsatisfied, the couple can begin to ask for what each wants from the other. For instance, I was raised by a single mother with nine children. She was a multitasker as well as emotionally remote. I was finally able to drop my frustration (the childhood reaction) and ask my wife, also a multitasker, to put down her knitting and talk to me. She said okay and I was able to begin to stop compulsively repeating my negative pattern.

Your husband can't open up as long as doing so doesn't seem safe. Unfortunately, his silence activates your childhood fear of being ignored or abandoned. This causes you to become invasive and cross his boundary: "Why don't you ever talk to me?"

Realizing this hopefully will allow you to back away, an action that will allow him to come forward.

" MY TAKE "

Dr. Farrell's answer speaks to the heart of the male/female divide. She is all about dotting the i's and crossing the t's when it comes to communicating feelings. He lacks the gene required for enthusiastic verbal unloading. Further widening the gulf, since the wife is likely his sole intimate confidant, it is that much scarier for him to bare his soul. However, in my work with couples, I have witnessed men's competitive instincts allowing them to overcome their less evolved verbal skills and let loose with that room-clearing rocket fire as well as, or better than, their wives.

Dr. Hendrix lasers in on a universal commonality which transcends gender—the need to repeat painful formative patterns in a largely unconscious quest to break free from this circular dead end. The more aware people become of the forces that shaped and to a certain extent still rule them, the less they need to cede their lives to the vagaries of intricate defense structures. The couple may set up a familiar dynamic but can opt to play a different hand—and get a different result.

Both experts give important real estate to an oft-forgotten truth: If it doesn't feel safe, a partner will stay tucked in his shell. Don't ask a spouse to open up if he will be running into sniper fire!

As Dr. Farrell points out, most people would step in front of a bullet if it would save their spouse. But it's the smaller dings and scratches, those daily digs, gripes, complaints, and plaints they inflict on their partner that take a slow but inevitable toll.

Wives: Ask not what you need from your husband but what he needs from you.

A tactic to consider—treat a life partner less like a spouse and more like a friend. This isn't about demoting the relationship. Rather, it's about promoting the idea that if a wife can emotionally step back a smidge from her husband, not regard his every thought, breath, and comment as something to which she deserves total 24/7 access, the marriage can benefit. Detach to attach.

People don't put as much pressure on friends to fulfill their every need. The stakes don't feel as high. Thus there are rarely Gestapo-like tactics: "Tell me what I want to hear or I will beat it out of you." Friends are less judgmental of what they hear from each other. They are better listeners and more impartial sounding boards.

Why can't my wife understand that I say things in anger I don't really mean?

MONA R. BARBERA, PhD:

The husband needs to understand his anger, what happens when rage overwhelms him. What does he actually say to himself, and is there a sequence of emotions he undergoes? The person typically experiences what occurs during the outburst as being consumed by anger and having no choice but to lash out. Later he might regret lashing out, so in order not to judge himself harshly he justifies the reasons for the anger.

Right now the wife either gets angry back or collapses, going into victimhood, thinking, "There's nothing I can do about this." Neither of these positions fosters dialogue. Rather, it results in loneliness and disconnection. Men and women want to be connected.

If the husband could slow it down and have awareness about each thing that happens during the anger episode, it would connect the couple. People alternate, experiencing various consuming emotions—anger, remorse, loneliness, and justification. It's like heading first to the salad station, then the pasta station, meats, then dessert. No part alone is the whole meal and no part alone is satisfying. Satisfaction, connection, comes from being transparent and able to express each emotion as he's experiencing it. Otherwise he's locked in the feeling and lost, apart from his partner. And his partner is apart from him.

When you're consumed by anger, your partner is your enemy. Being connected to and able to think through your anger means you can say, "I'm lost in my anger because you don't hear me when I speak and it's so uncomfortable not to be heard. It reminds me of my mother, who always listened to other people and not to me. I get angry and I lose it." If he can say this, something new will happen.

The husband, in this case, is uninterested in being reflective: "I'm angry. That's how it is." I would ask the wife, "Is there a way you can stay present when he's angry that leaves you calm and clear in your own experience?" This will relieve her of becoming lost in her own emotions. Such control is empowering and it helps the other person relax. He becomes more vulnerable and disclosing.

There's a flow waiting to happen between partners during an argument. It depends upon each being able to have a calm relationship with his or her individual experience.

SUE JOHNSON, EdD:

Perhaps if you can really take responsibility for your anger, sit down and talk to your wife about your deepest emotions, she can understand why you say these things. But when the most important person on the planet is getting angry and critical at you, it's almost impossible to act totally calm and detached. You are her precious one, and criticism from you is interpreted as a life or death matter. That's how it's coded in our brain: The person I love doesn't value me. Your wife's feelings of invalidation are further fed by the person she loves not responding to her feelings of hurt with reassurance. It's like someone yanking your security blanket.

Couples need to understand how they get caught up in this dreadful ancient dance, and the enormous impact they have on one another. As one person gets more and more angry and frustrated, the other feels more and more threatened, and withdraws. It's a horrible spiral, a whirlpool.

This is about attachment. Therapy is about learning to say to one another, "I'm getting angry right now and it's because I get so scared when you do such and such." One patient took a big risk, saying to her husband: "I told you the things I'm really scared about and you leaned back and rolled your head and said, 'I hurt too.' I felt so dismissed. I couldn't bear it."

The husband couldn't take it in. I slowed things down to help them focus on the core attachment instead of the Sturm und Drang surrounding them. I told the husband, "It's hard for you to hear your wife talk about her feeling scared because it's like there's a fog around you. All you can talk about is how angry you are. You can't really hear her."

Instead of wishing the wife could understand that he doesn't mean what he says in anger, he should try to help her see that although he might be angry for a moment, he still loves her. The softer feelings are underneath. When he's yelling and going berserk the wife can't see that he cares. Remember, for her it feels like life and death.

As people learn to clarify their emotions, they create new positive interactions of emotional responsiveness. If the husband can confide, "At those moments I get scared I don't matter to you. How could you love someone like me? Part of me sees your hurt but another part of me is still so angry and defensive it's hard for me to hear you," that's a whole different message than leaning back and rolling your eyes.

The purpose here is to help people step out of negative cycles and understand it is not the partner who is the enemy, but the negative patterns.

" MY TAKE "

Both therapists believe in breaking things down and learning to clarify the onrush of emotions rather than drowning in them.

Dr. Barbera outlines the benefits of slowing things down, trying to parse the feelings that flow through one during bouts of anger and hurt. I love the analogy of the salad bar. Who hasn't had that stuffed yet famished feeling resulting from gorging solely on empty calories? This is along the lines of yelling at a spouse just to make noise, and to feel one is not totally impotent. But screaming doesn't lead to feeling validated, connected, or happy—and odds are the spouse, the recipient of this rage, feels even worse.

Couples ignore Dr. Johnson's advice at their peril. Rather than seeking relief from the mental tsunami by mindlessly lashing out, a spouse should take responsibility for his or her actions. Couples think they are in control by working hard to be superior, which involves making each other insecure and off balance. But when they take the leap and let their partner into that soft, insecure place where they really live, reciprocation is possible. The best strategy is to be vulnerable with one another, to relinquish control by lowering defenses and potentially gaining a closer bond.

In the heat of the moment when one feels wronged, leading to an onrush of hurt, rage, fear, bitterness, resentment, and justification coursing through the veins, stop! Take a deep breath. Say, "This is how I've been reacting to conflict and anxiety-provoking situations since I was a kid. It's where I go. Maybe my spouse hasn't done anything to hurt me."

Taking that breath can help people unhook from their historic dysfunctional pattern and see the current situation from a place of logic. It's probably quite a different view! Couples should aim to be like rubber bands, snapping back to the present when they find themselves descending to the depths. The more reality-based they can be, the less likely they'll fall into the steps of that familiar and exhausting ancient dance.

FIELD REPORT

I stopped being bored with my marriage when I stopped being bored with myself. I expected my husband to entertain me and fill the void I felt inside. That wasn't in his job description, which he was smart enough to tell me. I switched jobs within my company, started an exercise program, and enrolled in a photography class. The result: Less time spent with Mark. Before I'd been nagging him to be with me every free minute! But the time together is choice because we both have something to contribute.

~ Ellen Simon, 34, Port Jefferson, New York

CHAPTER TWELVE

IF AT FIRST YOU DON'T SUCCEED

❧

Human beings are a strange and special lot. We complain pitifully about the travails of marriage, how much our ex didn't understand us, how he/she did us wrong. Yet hope springs eternal. We crave love enough to hold our noses and jump back into the marital waters. The crucial concerns that our relationship experts give clarity to in this chapter range from ways to truly learn from past mistakes to tactics to employ to keep a spouse's ex from poisoning a child against her stepparent.

How do you separate without anger and bitterness?

MELANIE WELLS, MA, LPC, LMFT:

The goal in moving forward with your life is to let go of the focus on the other person. Make it your mission in life to not ever be the kind of person who will be in that kind of relationship again. This means focusing on your own complicity and responsibility so you don't feel like a victim—a fool, maybe, once you realize what you've done, but not a victim!

It's important to differentiate that you want to empower yourself rather than be bitter. If people can go serenely about the business of becoming healthier, things start falling into place. With self-focused energy you can light up the city of Dallas. There's no time for blame or anger toward your ex.

The same principle applies in cases where infidelity was involved. A man whose wife cheated typically blames himself, thinking he was deficient in some way. A woman in this predicament, however, will think the fault lies with her husband: "I won't be with that ass anymore!" It's incumbent on the person who's been cheated on to ask herself or himself, "What was this about?" The reality is two people together created an unhealthy relationship.

LAUREN H. ZANDER:

The reason divorce becomes so twisted in people's minds is that each individual wants to feel like the innocent one and blame his or her former spouse.

People don't change all that much. What changes is they stop tolerating the traits in their partner they once thought were cute. Perhaps you once thought your spouse's indecisiveness was fine. You enjoyed helping him finally come to a decision about which fork in the road to follow. But now you've got two kids and a crazy schedule, and his inability to make up his mind is infuriating—a major reason you can't abide being with him anymore.

So the way to melt the vindictiveness you feel is to understand how you're the one who has changed. You're blaming your mate for something that he or she has been doing since you first met. Or maybe there was some agreement between the two of you that was never verbalized as such: When we got married you were so good looking and now you're fat! You can't voice this, but you feel betrayed. However, it's essential to own your part in the relationship's demise, which means owning your own bad traits; owning your imperfections.

If you can "get" that you prefer to scapegoat and blame your ex for your present unhappiness, you can begin not to have to do that. People are not as devastated about a relationship ending so much as they are terrified about what comes next. There is crazy fear about how to deal with money, find a date, and deal with the children. So part of the needing to drag out the divorce and hold on to the anger is to avoid getting to the next stage. Going to war means you can delay dealing with the unknown. Alternately, taking accountability for why you are in your current situation ultimately leads to a quiet place. It becomes easier.

The anger and bitterness did not happen overnight. It's the result of years of disconnect between the two of you. If you can understand how things got this way and that you're equally culpable, you can begin to forgive. If you prefer not to forgive and to stay at war, odds are you have learned nothing and will wreck your next marriage as well.

" MY TAKE "

The key point here, according to both experts, is to make a conscious decision to stop wallowing in the glorious muck of self-righteousness and start taking responsibility. As Wells stresses, this may involve temporarily feeling like a fool, but so long as one learns from the experience, there is evolution and less of a likelihood of making the same mistakes again. I also like the therapist's point that this strategy applies to cases of infidelity as well. Even if one partner did the deed, the other one helped get the marriage to the point where the union was vulnerable to such a rift.

Zander's main premise is also well-founded. It's not so likely that one's spouse has changed but rather that the mutual idiosyncrasies have little by little, brick by brick, eroded the relationship to the point where the differences between the couple are irreconcilable. And the main reason to forgive is not necessarily to let the mate off the hook (though that's a nice by-product), but because until angst and anger are discharged, people are not truly free to move on.

At the beginning of the workshops I conduct as an ancillary to my book *Love Lessons from Bad Breakups*, I stride onstage carrying a large suitcase. I tell the audience I am not heading to the airport at the conclusion of the evening; rather, the valise is a symbol of all the baggage we cart with us from bad relationship to bad relationship if we don't unpack between trips. If our MO is to keep blaming all our problems on other people, we will continually be emotionally weighted down and make the same mistakes. I open the bag, show the crowd the small change purse tucked inside, and say, "This is all that's left when we truly unpack our bags. It's barely carryon and not enough to keep us from being open to a new, more nourishing love."

I'm getting married for the fourth time and yes, I'm nervous. How can I make sure this one sticks?

HELEN DAHLHAUSER:

I would suggest this person make sure she's done individual psychological work before taking the plunge again. Does she know what her issues are? For instance, if she grew up in an abusive atmosphere she might be marrying the same person over and over, meaning she is repeating the pattern of her childhood. Each subsequent husband may have a different hair color, but it's the same person.

Another important piece: She should realize she is attractive to the opposite sex. Yes, there have been mistakes, but as long as she takes a look at her part and regroups, she can feel proud of herself versus judgmental. For instance, I have a patient on her fourth marriage. She had experienced shame and embarrassment over her history, but has worked hard and this marriage is successful.

It's also crucial that this woman and her fiancé do premarital counseling to make sure they're on the same page. Should she marry? As long as she behaves from a place of integrity and knows that this relationship is what she truly wants, it is a step forward.

MELANIE WELLS, MA, LPC, LMFT:

A person in this situation needs to be very self-aware about his or her role in the failures. In my practice I spend a lot of time listening to patients complaining about their ex-spouses. They use words like "abusive," "controlling," and "mean." I hear these words a lot, especially from patients who've been married a few times. They come to therapy to talk about how they keep picking the wrong partner.

I get them to work toward becoming a different person. I start by asking them to draw a line down the middle of a page. I have them put their most recent ex's name on the top of the left-hand column and then underneath that, list all the terrible things about him or her. In no time flat they come up with fifteen to twenty items: invasive, mean to my child, and so on. On the other side of the page I have them put their name and list all the corresponding traits that made the relationship possible. For instance, if she's invasive, he has poor boundaries. If he's mean to her kids, she's willing to tolerate that. I have them take a long, hard look at the list, read it aloud, and then tear it down the middle. I have them throw away the half about their former partner.

The one constant in all their failed marriages is themselves. From that point on, I don't let them talk about the ex. Oh, they can talk about a situation; for instance, "He was mean to me in front of my friends and I was so embarrassed. We left early." I make them reword it to, "He was mean to me in front of my friends and rather than ask him to leave I left with him, therefore protecting him from the consequences of his actions."

Each half of the engaged couple should separately make a list about their past relationships. This helps them see the way they unconsciously function in relationships over time. It is especially important to do if you've got a big body count in your wake!

" MY TAKE "

Some solid advice is offered here. Dahlhauser's point that a person can legally have four marriages under his or her belt, but emotionally only one, is apt. Keep mindlessly sticking a hand into the fire; it will still burn. Undergoing premarital counseling is also a wise move. A pre-nup might not hurt either!

I love the exercise Wells has her patients do geared toward making them look at their role in their failed marriages. Society teaches citizens to proudly take ownership of cars, houses, even microwave ovens. Put your John or Joan Hancock on the charge slip and take it home. However, it's not instilled in people to do something much harder—take ownership of actions. By having her patients make a list and then throw away the sheet containing the "proof" of all the bad things inflicted on them, Wells is forcing them to break free from the "poor, poor pitiful me, aren't I a cute victim" cycle that is destroying their lives.

Once a person can be comfortable with himself or herself rather than running from negative, confusing emotions to the distraction of a new partner, he or she is much more likely to make decisions such as remarriage from a place of strength and desire rather than desperation and fear.

My wife and I live with her eight-year-old son from her first marriage. This is my first marriage. We have no children of our own. Sometimes I feel jealous of the love she has for her child. Is this normal, or am I a terrible person?

BRENDA RODSTROM, LCSW:

You are not a terrible person, and this is totally normal.

Here's the quick and dirty: In a single-parent household, the parent and child form an incredibly strong team. Enter the stepparent, who, while a strong member of the husband/wife team at this juncture, is only a small part of the parent/child team. He's going to feel left out and jealous. This will subside over time. I advise stepparents to make sure that in the beginning they give their spouse and child enough alone time. If they can freely give that space, they will ultimately be much more welcome in the household.

Another important task is to develop your own relationship with your stepchild based on whatever common interests you can find. In the child's eyes you then become your own person and not just an interloper.

Since you don't have a child it's hard to understand the bond between your wife and her son. It's unconditional. You don't divorce a child. But a wife's love for her husband can be conditional. That's just reality.

Something that might ease your discomfort: Understand it is possible that remarrying has caused tremendous guilt for your wife. During the divorce she suffered and her child suffered, but in finding you she stopped suffering and began glowing. She's happy, but aware her child is not. He might like you, but it's not the way he feels about his father. So the mother will feel obliged to give him a little extra time and attention to alleviate his fears about what this new marriage will mean.

If a stepparent can understand what's going on in his partner's mind and in the child's—a lot of jealousy!—the situation becomes easier to bear.

Barbra Williams Cosentino, LCSW, RN:

Stop judging yourself. We all have a huge range of emotions that are not nice. In fact, it's wonderful that you can admit those feelings. As some wise person said, when you name it you contain it. Thus acknowledging to yourself and even to your wife that at times you feel jealous can be helpful.

Don't confide this to her in a blaming way, as in, "You spend so much time with him that it makes me feel bad." Instead use "I" sentences, "When I see you holed up for hours with Jake I feel lonely." Verbalizing your innermost emotions and having someone accept them can ease the sense that something is terribly wrong with you.

It's also important to pinpoint things that are lacking in the relationship. Is what you are feeling due to marital issues that would be present even if the child wasn't in the house? For example, do you feel that your wife doesn't show any interest in hearing details of your day? You might think this is because she is so focused on the child that you're lost in the shuffle. But the case might be that she just isn't a good listener.

The point here is not to make the child a scapegoat. Ask your wife for what you want, but also try to develop your own relationship with the boy. Do things with him that don't involve his mother. The more you're able to have loving feelings toward him, the less you'll feel he's taking his mother away from you.

" MY TAKE "

According to these experts, the transition to stepparenthood can be like emotional root canal minus Novocain. One needs to develop a strong ego to weather the feeling of not mattering to a new spouse. Rodstrom's tough-love point is to buck up and accept that a parent's love for a child is unconditional. I also endorse her suggestion to empathize with the wife's and stepchild's mindsets. They are going through a tough time as well.

Which leads to Williams Cosentino's excellent tip: Rather than bottle up feelings, in a non-blaming, sincere manner the stepparent should let his or her spouse in on what is going on. This should not be done with an expectation that the parent will stop catering to the child, but because it is crucial that couples share feelings and work toward compromises. An excellent one is suggested by both experts: Develop a relationship with the tyke.

The wife should handle the heavy lifting, meaning this is not the time for the husband to take a major role in disciplining her child. Since the boy seems shut down around his stepfather, it could be tempting to show who is in charge: "Hey, don't ignore me. When I say it's time to go to bed, hop to." This can serve to further alienate the child and upset the spouse as well.

And don't be ashamed to reach out for support. Check out the National Stepfamily Resource Center (*www.stepfamilies.info*). It has fact sheets, lists of state-by-state support groups, and more.

I think my husband's first wife is poisoning their ten-year-old against me. How can I get this little girl to not think I'm a devil with horns?

Carolyn Gerard, MA, MFT:

In a difficult divorce situation, what works is keeping the focus on the children. Thus this woman should concentrate on building a healthy, nurturing relationship with the child and to rise above the chatter from the ex-wife. This is a co-parenting issue. The stepmother's goal is to provide a role model of a responsible parent for the little girl.

To make this happen, the woman needs to work out her negative feelings about her husband's wife and not feel in competition with her. Thus it's imperative to have a solid relationship with her husband, to express feelings such as, "I want to feel close to your daughter but I think your ex is poisoning her against me." She needs the husband's reassurance that he is on her side. At some point he has to talk to his ex, saying something like, "I'm trying to make a go of this and what you're telling our daughter isn't in her best interest. You're always going to be her mother. Let's get beyond this." If that doesn't help, the couple together must do their best to rise above the bickering.

When the child brings up negative comments to her step-mother, such as, "My mother says you're this or that," the adult should not attack back. The disciplining is the father's responsibility. He needs to set guidelines for his child so it is clear she will always have her mother but is a part of a loving blended family: "This is your stepmother, and in our home we treat each other with respect. If there's something you need to talk about, let's do it."

It can take some time for the daughter to come to terms with the situation. In the meantime the stepmother needs a solid support system of friends and family so she can vent about the junk coming up.

RON MUCHNICK, PhD, AND SHERRI MUCHNICK, PhD:

The conflict between the parents does not always end with the divorce and can permeate their dealings with the children. The non-custodial parent, in this case the father, should not dwell on what the other parent is saying but rather concentrate on making the time the child spends with him and his wife positive. The understanding should be that the husband takes a lead role in disciplining his daughter but his wife is present when it is happening so there is a visual of her in the communication. If the couple is unified it's harder for the child to find the opening to drive the tank through.

The stepparent has to try for a broader view and not personalize the things the stepchild is saying. The child is part of a larger family "system," and it's possible she's being pushed to act out. We believe that over time, it is possible for the stepmother's actions to override the harsh reputation she is being given by the child's mother. The stepmother can't control what is being said about her, but if she continues to act in a caring, loving manner the child will begin to see that the things she is being fed about her father's wife aren't being borne out. Consequently the little girl will almost be forced to challenge these beliefs.

So the best advice is for this woman to take responsibility for her actions. If she allows herself to become angry at her husband, his former spouse, the little girl, all the people in this expanded family system of which she is now a part, she becomes the woman being described by the girl's mother. When the child says, "You can't tell me what to do. You're not my mother," she can calmly respond, "I'm not your mother, and it can be upsetting when I tell you to do things like clean your room." In other words, be direct and honest but leave space for the child's feelings. It's about being in control in how you respond versus being controlled by your emotions.

" MY TAKE "

The experts are united in their view that the stepmother needs to rise above the "junk," as Gerard puts it, and place the child's needs first. Both also assert, rightly, that the heavy lifting on the discipline front is better handled by the girl's father.

Gerard also stresses the importance of stepmom communicating her feelings and needs to her husband but having a support system available for venting purposes. Use the latter for the heavy lifting on the venting front. Endlessly, vituperatively "whipping" his ex can tax the marriage. More important, she doesn't want to appear to criticize his darling offspring. Calling little Tara spoiled, vindictive, a chip off the old block, and so on is something best directed to ears that are biased toward the stepmom's side.

The suggestion from Dr. Ron Muchnick and Dr. Sherri Muchnick that the stepmother take responsibility for her own actions is dead-on. Being reactive to the little girl's accusations that the stepmom is evil incarnate will only confirm the beliefs hammered into the child's head by her mother. Taking the high road obviously involves having lots of patience and fortitude, which goes back to the necessity of having a good support system.

Another tip to help the stepmother overcome feelings of resentment and hostility toward the little girl for making her feel unwanted in her own home is to put herself in the child's place; to remember being ten and feeling that something or someone was threatening her sense of well-being. The woman can enlist an old friend and/or sibling or her mother to remind her of how vulnerable, adrift, and self-focused she felt back then. Certainly family members will be pleased to remind her how impossible she was to be around, and that happily, it was a stage she grew out of. So, with displays of love and patience, can the stepdaughter.

FIELD REPORT

Buddy and I are both on our third marriage and living with three young teens—two his, one mine. For the first six months his younger son and my daughter did not get along at all! They lied, pitted my husband and me against each other, and wouldn't share food. It was ridiculous, so Buddy and I sat them down and set boundaries. We said, "From now on, if you have a problem with each other you can't go to your own parent, but to the parent of the kid you're mad at." Our children initially felt abandoned by us and tried every manipulation tactic in the book. But we were consistent and now, at eleven and twelve, they're best friends and go to bat for one another with the outside world.

~Cathy Oakes, 52, Columbia, Tennessee

LASTING LOVE

Russell and Norma LeBlanc
Reading, Massachusetts, married
thirty-eight years

"We laugh all the time."

Get out the hankies. It's 1968. Handsome twenty-three-year-old soldier meets pretty high school graduate (the ink was still wet on the girl's diploma!) and sweeps her off her feet. Six months later said soldier is dispatched to Korea for ROTC training. He is gone thirteen months, thankfully never seeing active duty in Vietnam.

The two mailed letters once a week and exchanged tapes made with cassette recorders. Remember them? There were occasional static-filled $12-a-minute phone calls as well.

Norma says, "I was young but the oldest of six, so mature for my age. I was never into the bar scene."

Russell adds, "Having no physical contact for so many months—our attraction was a huge distraction!—made it easier to get to know each other." Think *The Shop Around the Corner*, without the anonymity.

Aware that Norma would be spending Christmas Eve with his parents, he mailed an engagement ring to their house, asking them to give the gift to his beloved. They married two weeks after he returned to the States.

The courtship was super-romantic, made for the movies. The marriage has had its trials. Norma sighs, "There were huge fertility issues—years of workups and procedures at great emotional and financial expense. It takes over your life. After fifteen years of marriage we finally said, 'The heck with it. Let's stop trying.'" Almost instantly Norma, then thirty-four, became pregnant with their daughter, Nicole.

Eight years later Norma's sister lost custody of her son Shaun, amid allegations of alcohol and spousal abuse. The LeBlancs became foster parents and subsequently endured five difficult years (filled with lawyers, social workers, and uncertainty) before they were permitted to adopt the boy.

At the height of the custody trauma, Norma's mother was diagnosed with Alzheimer's. Norma sighs, "There were tough times. Russell handled things better than me. He was very patient and supportive."

Russell rebuts, "I didn't do anything special."

Norma rebuts the rebut: "He's very diplomatic."

A high priority has always been to stay connected. When Russell's real estate business forced him to travel, sometimes being away three or four nights a week, the couple turned his homecomings into little celebrations. Norma laughs, "I'd wait up for him with a glass of wine. He'd come through the door carrying flowers, even though sometimes he'd flown all night on the redeye."

When the travel eased, they commenced a pattern of regular Saturday-night dates. These were sacred, an unbreakable ritual. Russell says, "We see a lot of younger parents totally focused on their kids and think, 'Hey, you need to pay attention to each other.'"

There have been fights, but the couple make a point not to hang on to irritation and anger. They both insist, "You've got to treat each other with courtesy."

However, there is an upside to disagreements, according to Russell. "The make-up sex is great!" Norma spills another secret to their longevity: "We laugh all the time."

She lets her husband have the last word. "We're both by-products of successful relationships. It was like growing up in a classroom with the subject being, 'How to interact in a healthy way.' We were fortunate to learn good communication skills."

Mutual courtesy, shared goals, making time for one another, constant laughter, good communication—that's a pretty good recipe for a happy marriage.

Appendix A

GUIDELINES FOR CHOOSING A MARRIAGE COUNSELOR

~ ❦ ~

Many couples do not opt for counseling until they are in crisis. Typically one person wants to separate, and therapy is a last-ditch attempt to save the relationship. However, couples therapy can be helpful at any stage of the game. Its purpose is to help couples learn and implement communication-building tools; work through impasses with a problem-solving mindset rather than a "my way or the highway" attitude; handle conflict in a healthier manner; deal with crises (such as an extramarital affair, domestic violence), sexual issues, and changing roles (among them parenthood, empty nest); and develop a more intimate connection.

WHAT TO EXPECT

During the sessions the couple typically are led to examine their childhoods to gain an understanding of how they turn their partners into their parents to a certain extent and on a subconscious level. Counseling is goal-oriented, often short term, and can involve "homework" between sessions. Finally, the role of the counselor is not necessarily to save the relationship but to help both partners understand and illuminate to themselves and to each other the goals in the marriage . . . even if a goal turns out to be learning how to separate in a healthy manner.

WHAT TO DO

It is crucial to carefully check the education, credentials, and experience of your potential therapist. Does he or she have experience in treating your problems? Most states require advanced training. Many counselors are trained specifically as licensed marriage and family therapists (LMFTs). Find out if your therapist belongs to a professional association such as the American Association for Marriage and Family Therapy (AAMFT). Ask about fees, insurance coverage, the average time frame of therapy, and other pertinent questions.

There is a certain chemistry that exists between a therapist and his or her patient(s). It is essential that both partners feel safe in the room and that their therapist is objective yet on both their sides. Marriage counseling is not a miracle pill, but with work, sweat, tears, and commitment it can work miracles.

EXPERTS' BIOS, BOOKS, AND MARRIAGE-SAVING TIPS

Keith Ablow, MD

"America's Psychiatrist"; couples counselor; best-selling author,
Living the Truth: Transform Your Life Through the Power of
Insight and Honesty.
www.livingthetruth.com

PHILOSOPHY: *Every conflict is an opportunity for greater intimacy.
If, for instance, a husband can examine why he has the need to be
controlling—it goes back to his family of origin—and the wife looks
at why she lacks the self-esteem to be equal, they can begin to share
power more equally.*

Isadora Alman

*Marriage and relationship therapist; board-certified sexologist;
author; syndicated sex and relationship columnist.*
www.askisadora.com

PHILOSOPHY: *Much more important than whether we can put slot
A into slot B—mechanical sexual techniques—is to develop comfort in
communication. I'll ask couples if they're comfortable in asking for what
they want and they'll say, "Oh, yes." Then I'll say, "Can you refuse what
you're not comfortable doing?" and they'll go, "Oh, uh, no."*

JONATHAN ALPERT

Psychotherapist; specializes in relationship and sexual problems.
www.jonathanalpert.com

PHILOSOPHY: *It's imperative to argue in a healthier manner. I suggest thirty-minute time-outs during which you stop and ask yourself, "What do I really want to accomplish? To resolve the problem or hurt my partner?"*

BERNARD J. BACA, PHD, LCSW

Marital/couples therapist; more than twenty-one years' experience; certified Imago Therapist.
www.indiana-imago.com

PHILOSOPHY: *My job is to help couples see they're in the correct marriage. Otherwise they'll divorce, find somebody else, and in a couple of years be in the same situation.*

MONA R. BARBERA, PHD

Psychologist; specializes in couples; author, Bring Yourselves to Love: How Couples Can Turn Disconnection into Intimacy.
www.monabarbera.com

PHILOSOPHY: *People alternate between being consumed by guilt, anger, or disconnection. These feelings confuse them and take them away from their partner. If they can talk about these feelings instead of being consumed by them it's like a cleansing.*

LEE H. BAUCOM, PHD

Family and marriage counselor; twenty years' experience.
www.savethemarriage.com

PHILOSOPHY: *Instead of trying to make your partner see the world the way you see it, ask him or her to help you understand his or her point of view. You don't have to agree, but there is room for differences.*

SHEILA BENDER, PhD

Psychologist; coauthor, The Energy of Belief: Psychology's Power Tools to Focus Intention and Release Blocking Beliefs. ***www.energyofbelief.com***

PHILOSOPHY: *Couples develop protective, reflexive responses, making the same moves time and again. There needs to be a shift; otherwise, they're enabling each other to stay inside their comfort zones.*

RABBI YEHUDA BERG

Kabbalistic teacher providing counsel to hundreds of couples; author, The Spiritual Rules of Engagement: How Kabbalah Can Help Your Soul Mate Find You.

PHILOSOPHY: *I have couples take a break from trying to solve the problem together, to stop choking each other and do some inner focusing. This helps them look at their own complicity, and to stop being so reactive to their partner.*

LEANNE BRADDOCK, MEd, MA

Marital and family therapist; author, Taming the Dragon Within: How to Be the Mother-in-Law You've Always Wanted.

PHILOSOPHY: *There is no point addressing any of the issues a couple brings in unless they talk respectfully to and really listen to each other.*

STEPHANIE BUEHLER, MSW, PSYD, CST

Psychologist; sex therapist; internationally known for her expertise in relationships, sexuality, and intimacy; director of the Buehler Institute.

www.thebuehlerinstitute.com

PHILOSOPHY: *Couples have unrealistic expectations that skyrockets should go off day after day, year after year. Yet they've been having sex in the same position for the last twenty years—hello! They spend more time discussing the breed of dog they want than what would be fulfilling sexually.*

JOHN BURKE MEALY, PHD

Psychologist; more than thirty years in practice.

www.counselorswithcompassion.com

PHILOSOPHY: *Having positive experiences as a couple is the backbone of a good relationship. That's what gives them the resources to deal with difficult times.*

RENÉE A. COHEN, PHD

Clinical and forensic psychology; working with couples thirty years.

PHILOSOPHY: *Each person should look at what his or her spouse brings to the table: "Does he or she enhance my life, make me a better person, or do I wind up feeling brought down?" What do they think needs to be improved, and how available are they to work on the relationship?*

JOHN CURTIS, PHD

Former family and marriage counselor; consultant; author, Marriage Built to Last: 9 Steps to Life-Long Love!

www.marriagebuilttolast.org

PHILOSOPHY: *Couples should look at growing their marriage as they would growing a business. They need a vision statement, job descriptions, and regular performance appraisals.*

HELEN DAHLHAUSER

Relationship therapist; author, Before You Leave: End with Love. **www.before-you-leave.com**

PHILOSOPHY: *If each person can learn to show deep integrity, admit to his or her shortcomings, and come from a place of mutual respect, the relationship will be greatly enhanced.*

WILLIAM J. DOHERTY, PhD

Psychologist; marriage and family therapist; author, Take Back Your Marriage: Sticking Together in a World That Pulls Us Apart; *cofounder of the National Registry of Marriage-Friendly Therapists.* **www.drbilldoherty.org**

PHILOSOPHY: *Any couple can have a reasonably successful marriage if they both put energy into it, and when a problem comes up both work on it.*

PAUL DUNION, EdD, LPC

Counseling psychotherapist for twenty-seven years; author, Shadow Marriage: A Descent into Intimacy. **www.pauldunion.com**

PHILOSOPHY: *I focus couples out of victimhood and toward self-empowerment. Instead of complaining how badly they're treated they need to realize, "Oh, I hold a grudge and get passive-aggressive."*

Bonnie Eaker Weil, PhD

Psychology Today *and* New York Magazine *called her one of America's best-known relationship experts; author of the bestsellers* Make Up, Don't Break Up: Rescue Your Relationship and Rekindle Your Romance; Adultery, the Forgivable Sin; *and* Financial Infidelity: Seven Steps to Conquering the #1 Relationship Wrecker.
www.doctorbonnie.com

PHILOSOPHY: *I ask couples to pick at least one behavior each will simultaneously work on changing. These behaviors are written down and each person gets a copy and coaches his or her spouse on those changes using positive reinforcement versus blame: "Do I have permission to ask you to put your dirty clothes in the hamper when I see them on the floor?" Both are coached to show gratitude when the other manages the task.*

Elizabeth Einstein, MA/LMFT

Marriage and family therapist; stepfamily trainer and consultant.
www.stepfamilyliving.com

PHILOSOPHY: *I try to teach couples not to be frightened of crisis but rather to look at the possibilities within the crisis, the lessons they can learn.*

Warren Farrell, PhD

Couples' communication coach; author, Women Can't Hear What Men Don't Say *and* Why Men Are the Way They Are; *developer of the "Cinematic Immersion Method" to reprogram our biologically natural response to respond defensively to personal criticism from a loved one.*
www.warrenfarrell.com

PHILOSOPHY: *As a couple master the ability to handle personal criticism without feeling defensive, they begin to feel safe enough to handle their partner's honesty. This fosters the growth of the relationship.*

CAROLYN GERARD, MA, MFT

Marriage and family therapist.
www.Relationships4Life.com

PHILOSOPHY: *Couples come in, really missing the closeness they used to have. I slow them down to get beyond the, "He (she) did this to me" blame cycle and to focus on the underlying feelings, the fear and shame. The anger is typically their way of saving themselves from not feeling cared about.*

BARTON GOLDSMITH, PHD

Award-winning psychotherapist; works with couples on issues ranging from addiction and infidelity to trauma and abuse; author, Emotional Fitness for Couples: 10 Minutes a Day to a Better Relationship.
www.bartongoldsmith.com

PHILOSOPHY: *The object is preventive maintenance. Once a day have a ten-minute check-in. Do something lovely together. It could be watching a sunset or just holding hands. If you have a good ten minutes, you have a good life.*

JAY P. GRANAT, PHD

Psychotherapist; marriage and family therapist; more than twenty-four years of clinical experience.
www.stayinthezone.com

PHILOSOPHY: *There are always two levels—the problem the couple thinks is the issue and their underlying personality structure, meaning the "old tapes" they bring to the relationship. They need to develop insight, to quit playing those old tapes and stop having the same tantrums they did as a child when thwarted.*

JOHN GRAY, PHD

Internationally recognized expert in fields of communications and relationships; author of sixteen relationship books including Why Mars and Venus Collide: Improving Relationships by Understanding How Men and Women Cope Differently with Stress; *conducting personal growth seminars for more than thirty years.*

www.marsvenus.com

PHILOSOPHY: *The sexes are different. You can't expect your partner to automatically respond the way you want. A man is not just going to be romantic. But if a wife tells her husband three things she'd like him to do and asks him to arrange one of them, he'll arrange it. And a man needs to listen to a woman, let her talk, instead of trying to solve her problems.*

JANE GREER, DSW, LMFT

Nationally known marriage and family therapist; in private practice more than twenty years; author of many books including The Afterlife Connection: A Therapist Reveals How To Communicate with Departed Loved Ones *and* How Could You Do This To Me? Learning to Trust After Betrayal.

www.drjanegreer.com

PHILOSOPHY: *Negative patterns derail couples when they talk to each other about issues. They must learn to listen, empathize, and respond in nonaccusatory ways. When you're accepting and supportive, you promote compromise and caring.*

Scott Haltzman, MD

Couples counselor; author, The Secrets of Happily Married Men, The Secrets of Happily Married Women, *and* The Secrets of Happy Families.
www.DrScott.com

PHILOSOPHY: *Men and women are designed differently. We shouldn't be putting our energies toward changing our partner, getting him or her to be more like we are. Rather, we should put our energies toward understanding that difference and acting accordingly.*

Mary Hammond, MA

Counseling couples more than twenty-five years; author, Living Your Soul's Purpose: Wellness and Passion with Energy Psychology and Energy Medicine.

PHILOSOPHY: *Couples need to be passionate about some cause or belief that is greater than themselves—church, politics, raising their children, creating a garden on their land.*

Willard F. Harley, Jr., PhD

Nationally acclaimed clinical psychologist; marriage counselor; bestselling author, His Needs, Her Needs: Building an Affair-Proof Marriage.
www.marriagebuilders.com

PHILOSOPHY: *Couples need to keep depositing what I call love units, good feelings, into each other's Love Bank. Make too many withdrawals of love units and you create a negative balance, meaning your partner associates you with bad feelings.*

SUSAN HEITLER, PhD

Clinical psychologist; helping couples for more than twenty-five years; author of a book, workbook, and workshops called The Power of Two: Secrets to a Strong & Loving Marriage. *www.therapyhelp.com*

PHILOSOPHY: *If couples have poor conflict-resolution skills, they detour off the road to well-being and harmony to anger, depression, anxiety, and obsessive-compulsive or addictive behavior, such as workaholism or overeating. By learning skills for collaborative problem solving, the negative feelings go away. There are free downloads on my website.*

GAY HENDRICKS, PhD, AND KATHLYN HENDRICKS, PhD, ADTR

Cofounders of the Hendricks Institute and the Foundation for Conscious Living; have worked with thousands of couples; coauthored and authored many books including Conscious Loving: The Journey to Co-Commitment. *www.hendricks.com*

PHILOSOPHY: *Couples have to commit to being 100 percent in the relationship, not, "I'm willing to commit if my partner admits she's a bitch or stops drinking."*

HARVILLE HENDRIX, PhD

Clinical pastoral counselor; known internationally for his work with couples; co-created "Imago Relationship Therapy" and the concept of "conscious partnership" with wife Helen LaKelly Hunt, PhD, with whom he's coauthored nine books including Receiving Love: Transform Your Relationship by Letting Yourself Be Loved. *www.harvillehendrix.com*

PHILOSOPHY: *We are all interconnected. Having a judgmental thought creates a disturbance that will include you. Decide in advance the outcome you desire with your partner and then behave in a way to make that happen.*

KATHRYN JANUS

Advanced clinician in Imago Relationship Therapy; has worked with hundreds of couples over the past eighteen years.

PHILOSOPHY: *Rather than loving each other's potential, the person your mate can and should become, you need to love the person sitting across from you.*

SUE JOHNSON, EdD

One of the originators of Emotionally Focused Couples Therapy (EFT); director of the Ottawa (Canada) Couple and Family Institute; author, Hold Me Tight: Seven Conversations for a Lifetime of Love.
www.holdmetight.net

PHILOSOPHY: *The issue isn't how often a couple fights, but do they have the ability afterward to make up and connect emotionally? It's important to focus on the signals you send your partner and whether those signals pull your partner close or push him or her away.*

PHIL KIRSCHBAUM, LCSW

More than thirty years' experience as therapist; specializes in marital work; cofounder of Gurnee Counseling Center.
www.gurneecounselingcenter.com

PHILOSOPHY: *At the heart of a successful marriage is a friendship. If there is or has been a friendship, there is something to build on. If there hasn't been one, I'm not very optimistic.*

Diana Kirschner, PhD

> *Marital therapy expert on bringing marriages back to life; author,* Love in 90 Days: The Essential Guide to Finding Your Own True Love; *former director of the Institute for Comprehensive Family Therapy.*
> ***www.dianakirschner.com***

PHILOSOPHY: *The litmus test of a happy couple is that they are best friends with chemistry. I ask, "Would you be acting the way you do with your partner with your best friend?" The other thing I ask is, "If you were having an affair with your spouse, would you be wearing that ratty bathrobe or have your hair so raggedy it looks like you're homeless?"*

Judy Kuriansky, PhD

> *Marriage therapist; former host of the syndicated radio call-in show* Love Phones; *author,* Complete Idiot's Guide to a Healthy Relationship *and* Complete Idiot's Guide to Tantric Sex.

PHILOSOPHY: *If a couple thinks the relationship is over, they're not really committed to it. Any two people can make something work as long as they both really want it to. From there, every day can be a fresh start.*

Ella Lasky, PhD

> *Clinical psychologist; thirty years' experience with couples and family therapy.*

PHILOSOPHY: *One person is not the problem. It's how both people contribute to the issues between them.*

Pat Love, EdD

> *Past president of the International Association for Marriage and Family Counseling; faculty emeritus, Imago Institute for Relationship Therapy; best-selling author,* Hot Monogamy:

Essential Steps to More Passionate, Intimate Lovemaking *and* The Truth About Love: The Highs, the Lows, and How You Can Make It Last Forever; *coauthor,* How to Improve Your Marriage Without Talking About It: Finding Love Beyond Words.

www.patlove.com

PHILOSOPHY: *It's about connection, stupid. Beating your spouse over the head with what you want will accomplish the opposite of your desire. He or she will feel inadequate. Think connection, then say, "How can we work as a team?"*

Cloé Madanes, PhD, FAPA

Recognized internationally as an innovator in both family and grief therapy; president of the Robbins-Madanes Center for Strategic Intervention; author of six books that are classics in psychotherapy; coauthor, The Ultimate Relationship Program, *a "workshop in a box" designed to enhance couples' relationships.*

www.robbinsmadanes.com

PHILOSOPHY: *People will say, "I don't understand why my spouse is so mad at me. I give him/her everything." Yes, everything but what the spouse needed. One must begin to understand the needs of the spouse and how to satisfy them.*

Debra Mandel, PhD

Psychologist; more than twenty years' experience specializing in relationships; author; columnist.

www.drdebraonline.com

PHILOSOPHY: *The underlying issues often have to do with equality and power in the relationship—who has more decision-making power about money, vacation, how they spend time with the kids, who runs the household? Each partner wants to be soothed by the other but feels* *so devalued and wounded that he or she has no soothing capability left. They're all about "me," not "we."*

OLIVIA MELLAN

Money coach; psychotherapist; author, The Secret Language of Money.
www.moneyharmony.com

PHILOSOPHY: *Understand your partner's money personality. For example, one person might be a hoarder while the other is a risk-taker. Then figure out an action you can take once a day, week, etc., to practice being in your partner's world. Walk a half mile in his or her moccasins. Do what doesn't come naturally.*

CHRISTINE MORIARTY, CFP

More than twenty years' experience; dubbed "financial marriage therapist" by grateful clients.
www.moneypeace.com

PHILOSOPHY: *There needs to be a balance of financial responsibility for a couple to thrive; a shared responsibility. This means they must not make money decisions without their partner's knowledge.*

JOYCE MORLEY-BALL, EdD

Marriage and relationship therapist for more than twenty years; hosted radio talk show Love and Relationships; *author,* Seeds for the Harvest of a Lifetime: Increasing Self-Awareness, Self-Esteem, and Improving Relationships.
www.doctorjoyce.com

PHILOSOPHY: *Don't try to change someone else. People don't change. Go from blaming your spouse for everything that is wrong to taking responsibility for your actions.*

Ron Muchnick, PhD, and Sherri Muchnick, PhD

Marriage and family therapists; professors at Capella University.

PHILOSOPHY: *We ask the couple, "If a miracle happened and the issues you came to therapy about no longer concerned you, what would be different?" This allows the two to develop a shared vision of what their marriage can look like that would be fulfilling rather than focusing on the past.*

Linda Olson, PsyD

Clinical psychologist; more than twenty-five years' experience with couples.
www.americaslovedoctor.com

PHILOSOPHY: *Couples need to take emotional risks. If you go to the gym, it hurts. If you want a fabulous marriage, you have to push yourself to grow. It won't always be easy, but the rewards are unbelievable.*

Tania Paredes, LCSW, DCSW

Marital counselor; adjunct professor at the School of Social Work–Barry University.
www.taniaparedes.com

PHILOSOPHY: *Often people wait until things are very bad before communicating things that are wrong. It's important to say things like, "Lately I feel like we're not connecting." That way you can work on the problem before it becomes very serious.*

ESTHER PEREL

Marriage and family therapist; author of the bestseller Mating in Captivity: Reconciling the Erotic and the Domestic; *member of the American Family Therapy Academy and of the Society for Sex Therapy and Research.*
www.estherperel.com

PHILOSOPHY: *I do not impose my beliefs on couples; I try to allow them to be expansive. I ask, "What are you thinking about? Where do you draw the line? What do you consider secret? What are your expectations about marriage? Do you expect your partner to be your best friend, passionate lover, or person with whom you have a beautiful family life and respectful social position?"*

FRANK PITTMAN, MD

Family therapist; author of the classic Private Lies: Infidelity and Betrayal of Intimacy; *since 1962 has treated more than 1,500 couples.*

PHILOSOPHY: *Think in terms of how everything you do affects the marriage. Consider how you make your partner feel. Your anger is not likely to be helpful. It's a matter of being kind, having concern for the sensibility of others. Be kind if you expect the other person to be kind to you.*

SHARON M. RIVKIN, MA, MFT

Marriage and family therapist; conflict resolution expert; author, The First Argument: Cutting to the Root of Intimate Conflict.
www.sharonrivkin.com

PHILOSOPHY: *I tell people to look at their first argument to find the seeds of their core issue. For example, one husband didn't want to dance at their wedding. His refusal was rooted in not wanting to* *be embarrassed, but it triggered abandonment issues in the wife. The abandonment/shame dance continued for years until they understood their pattern.*

Brenda Rodstrom, LCSW

Founder of Stepfamily Dynamics Counseling and Coaching.
www.stepfamilydynamics.com

PHILOSOPHY: *Stepfamilies function very differently than nuclear families. Learn the differences. Go to websites such as the National Stepfamily Resource Center (www.stepfamilies.info). Understand each other through dialogue. Don't accuse. Ask, "I wonder why you spoil your child." He can answer, "I only see him once every two weeks."*

Don and Martha Rosenthal

Relationship counselors; founders of the Heartwork Center, which holds weekend couples' workshops; authors, Learning to Love: From Conflict to Lasting Harmony.
www.heartworkcenter.org

PHILOSOPHY: *We encourage couples to discern the purpose of their relationship. It may sound like a funny question, but it's a deep one. In the olden days the purpose may have been economic necessity. We propose an alternative purpose—intimacy as a spiritual path.*

Rebecca Roy, MA, MFT

Psychotherapist; specializes in relationship issues.
www.theindustrytherapist.com

PHILOSOPHY: *I look at a lot of underlying issues. Are there unresolved family of origin issues currently being played out? Is each spouse subconsciously expecting the other to fulfill a role?*

Alisa Ruby Bash, MA, MFTI

Marriage and family therapist.
www.alisaruby.com

PHILOSOPHY: *Being in a relationship does not mean couples should stop growing as individuals. Sometimes breaking up is a sign of growth.*

Karen Sherman, PhD

Psychologist; in private practice since 1982; specializes in relationships.
www.drkarensherman.com

PHILOSOPHY: *Learning to understand and validate each other rather than attack is crucial. If the wife makes a harsh statement—"When was the last time you brought me flowers?"—her meaning is, "I need to know I'm important to you." But he hears, "I'm not good enough."*

Stephen W. Simpson, PhD

Psychologist; specializes in relationships, anxiety, and sexual issues; coauthor, What Wives Wish Their Husbands Knew about Sex: A Guide for Christian Men.
www.stephenwsimpson.com

PHILOSOPHY: *The biggest thing missing when a couple has a conflict is empathy, the ability to understand something from the other person's perspective. When our partner does something we don't like we interpret it as an attack—he or she wants to hurt or control us. Our automatic reaction is to be frightened and attack back. Coming to understand this trap softens couples and improves their ability to communicate.*

BEVERLY SMALLWOOD, PhD

Psychologist; couples counselor for thirty years; founder of the Hope Center; author, This Wasn't Supposed to Happen to Me: 10 Make-or-Break Choices When Life Steals Your Dreams and Rocks Your World.
www.DrBevSmallwood.com

PHILOSOPHY: *Challenging the ways people think about their partners and their interactions is an essential part of healing. Couples often have distorted perceptions of situations based on things like their expectations of how things are supposed to be, their emotional habits, past relationships, and insecurities.*

MARION SOLOMON, PhD

Cofounder of the Lifespan Learning Institute, dedicated to the advanced training and application of research in individual, group, and family therapy; cowriting Love and War in Intimate Relationships.

PHILOSOPHY: *People come in thinking the problem is about sex or how they handle money. We talk about those issues, but what's really necessary is to talk about how they talk to each other and what they really want in an intimate relationship.*

STEVEN STOSNY, PhD

Marriage counselor; coauthor, How to Improve Your Marriage Without Talking about It: Finding Love Beyond Words; *founder of CompassionPower, programs created to reduce anger, violence, and resentment.*
www.compassionpower.com

PHILOSOPHY: *Couples need to make sure they're always attuned to what's most important. For most people it's their connection. Couples need to be able to get irritated with one another, say if a towel is left on the floor, without devaluing each other.*

BARBARA SWENSON, PHD

Clinical psychologist; marriage and family therapist for twenty-one years.

PHILOSOPHY: *The difficulties we have emotionally attaching as children often play out in adult relationships. I tell couples, "You have to understand your own issues and your partner's, and be more sensitive based on what each of you had a hard time with growing up."*

MICHELE WEINER-DAVIS, MSW

Internationally renowned marriage therapist; bestselling author, Divorce Busting *and* The Sex-Starved Marriage: A Couple's Guide to Boosting Their Marriage Libido; *director of the Divorce Busting Center.*
www.divorcebusting.com

PHILOSOPHY: *Couples expect a therapist to pass a verdict on who's right and who's wrong. They're both right. The question is, can they find a way to give to one another in a creative way although they have diametrically opposed needs?*

MELANIE WELLS, MA, LPC, LMFT

Marriage and family therapist; founder of Lifeworks Counseling Associates.
www.lifeworkscounseling.net/mel.php

PHILOSOPHY: *I'm not in the business of saving marriages, but helping individuals differentiate from one another and learn to function in a healthy way. Sometimes a relationship survives and sometimes it shouldn't.*

BARBRA WILLIAMS COSENTINO, LCSW, RN

Psychotherapist; twenty-five years of experience working with couples.

PHILOSOPHY: *There's a belief you should be able to talk about all your feelings with your partner. That's not true. That's what friends and journals are for. There are things better off not shared with your partner. It's important to protect his or her areas of vulnerability, to not hit him or her below the belt.*

LESLIEBETH WISH, EDD

Psychologist; social worker; has worked with thousands of couples.
www.lovevictory.com

PHILOSOPHY: *Each couple is part of a multigenerational "system." It is important to look at their parents' marriage and history. That is where they've learned about love, life, men, women, marriage, trust, hurt, and strength.*

LAUREN H. ZANDER

Couples coach; founder and chairman of the Handel Group Private Coaching Company.
www.handelgroup.com

PHILOSOPHY: *Ask yourself, "Did I marry my mother or my father?" You married one so you could repeat the patterns of the other. It's important for couples to recognize and have a sense of humor about this in order to stop picking on each other and help one another overcome these traits.*

Michael D. Zentman, PhD

Clinical psychologist; working with couples thirty-nine years; director of the Postgraduate Program in Marriage & Couple Therapy at Adelphi University.

PHILOSOPHY: *We choose our partners based on early relationships with our parents. This provides a blueprint for all our relationships. Therapy gives couples the opportunity to rework the blueprint to turn out a better result not by trying to change our partner, but to reflect on ourselves and the issues we bring.*

INDEX